THE CLEVELAND WAY AND
THE YORKSHIRE WOLDS WAY

About the Author

Paddy Dillon is a prolific walker and guidebook writer, with almost 100 guidebooks to his name and contributions to 40 other titles. He has written extensively for many different outdoor publications and has appeared on radio and television. Paddy uses a tablet computer to write his route descriptions while walking. His descriptions are therefore precise, having been written at the very point at which the reader uses them.

Paddy is an indefatigable long-distance walker who has walked all of Britain's National Trails and several major European trails. He lives on the fringes of the Lake District and has walked, and written about walking, in every county throughout the British Isles. He has led guided walks and walked throughout Europe, as well as in Nepal, Tibet, Korea, Africa and the Rocky Mountains of Canada and the US. Paddy is a member of the Outdoor Writers and Photographers Guild and President of the Backpackers Club.

Other Cicerone guides by the author

Glyndwr's Way
Mountain Walking in Mallorca
The GR5 Trail
The GR20 Corsica
The Great Glen Way
The Irish Coast to Coast Walk
The Mountains of Ireland
The National Trails
The North York Moors
The Pennine Way
The Reivers Way
The South West Coast Path
The Teesdale Way (Martin Collins; updated by Paddy Dillon)
The Wales Coast Path
Trekking in Greenland – the Arctic Circle Trail
Trekking in Mallorca
Trekking in the Alps (contributing author)

Trekking in the Canary Islands
Walking and Trekking in Iceland
Walking in County Durham
Walking in Menorca
Walking in Sardinia
Walking in the Azores
Walking in the Isles of Scilly
Walking in the North Pennines
Walking on Arran
Walking on Gran Canaria
Walking on Guernsey
Walking on Jersey
Walking on La Gomera and El Hierro
Walking on Lanzarote and Fuerteventura
Walking on La Palma
Walking on Madeira
Walking on Malta
Walking on Tenerife

THE CLEVELAND WAY AND THE YORKSHIRE WOLDS WAY

by Paddy Dillon

JUNIPER HOUSE, MURLEY MOSS,
OXENHOLME ROAD, KENDAL, CUMBRIA LA9 7RL
www.cicerone.co.uk

Printed in China on responsibly sourced paper on behalf of Latitude Press Ltd
A catalogue record for this book is available from the British Library.
All photographs are by the author unless otherwise stated.

Updates to this Guide

While every effort is made by our authors to ensure the accuracy of guide-books as they go to print, changes can occur during the lifetime of an edition. Any updates that we know of for this guide will be on the Cicerone website (www.cicerone.co.uk/823/updates), so please check before planning your trip. We also advise that you check information about such things as transport, accommodation and shops locally. Even rights of way can be altered over time. We are always grateful for information about any discrepancies between a guidebook and the facts on the ground, sent by email to updates@cicerone.co.uk or by post to Cicerone, Juniper House, Murley Moss, Oxenholme Road, Kendal, LA9 7RL.

Register your book: To sign up to receive free updates, special offers and GPX files where available, register your book at www.cicerone.co.uk.

Front cover: Looking from Cringle Moor to Carlton Bank on Stage 3 of the Cleveland Way

CONTENTS

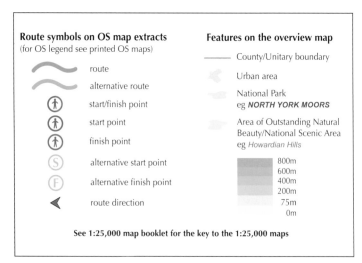

Route symbols on OS map extracts
(for OS legend see printed OS maps)

route

alternative route

start/finish point

start point

finish point

alternative start point

alternative finish point

route direction

Features on the overview map

County/Unitary boundary

Urban area

National Park
eg **NORTH YORK MOORS**

Area of Outstanding Natural
Beauty/National Scenic Area
eg *Howardian Hills*

800m
600m
400m
200m
75m
0m

See 1:25,000 map booklet for the key to the 1:25,000 maps

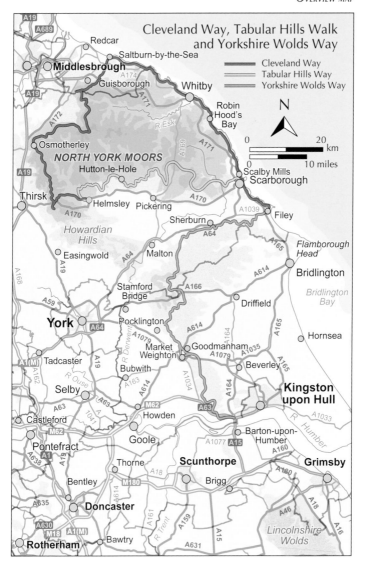

Cleveland Way, Tabular Hills Walk and Yorkshire Wolds Way

— Cleveland Way
— Tabular Hills Way
— Yorkshire Wolds Way

Cleveland Way Trek Planner

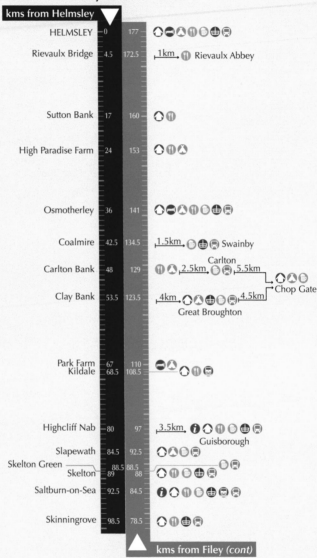

kms from Helmsley

	kms from Helmsley	kms from Filey	
HELMSLEY	0	177	
Rievaulx Bridge	4.5	172.5	1km → Rievaulx Abbey
Sutton Bank	17	160	
High Paradise Farm	24	153	
Osmotherley	36	141	
Coalmire	42.5	134.5	1.5km → Swainby
Carlton Bank	48	129	2.5km → Carlton 5.5km → Chop Gate
Clay Bank	53.5	123.5	4km → Great Broughton 4.5km
Park Farm	67	110	
Kildale	68.5	108.5	
Highcliff Nab	80	97	3.5km → Guisborough
Slapewath	84.5	92.5	
Skelton Green	88.5	88.5	
Skelton	89	88	
Saltburn-on-Sea	92.5	84.5	
Skinningrove	98.5	78.5	

kms from Filey *(cont)*

kms from Helmsley *(cont)*

Location	kms from Helmsley	kms from Filey	Facilities
Staithes	106.5	70.5	⌂ ⛺ ⑪ ⊜ ⊕ ⊟
Port Mulgrave	109	68	1km ⌂ ⛺ ⊜ ⊕ ⊟
Runswick Bay	111.5	65.5	⌂ ⛺ ⑪ ⊟
Loop Wyke	116	61	1km ⌂ ⊜ Slapewath
Sandsend	120	57	⌂ ⑪ ⊜ ⊕ ⊟
Whitby	125	52	ⓘ ⌂ ⊜ ⛺ ⑪ ⊜ ⊕ ⊟ ⊟
Saltwick Bay	127	50	⑪ ⊕
Maw Wyke Hole	131.5	45.5	⑪
Robin Hood's Bay	136.5	40.5	⌂ ⑪ ⊜ ⊕ ⊟
Boggle Hole	137.5	39.5	
Ravenscar	142	35	⌂ ⑪ ⊜ ⊟
Hayburn Wyke	148.5	28.5	⌂ ⊜
Old Scalby Mills	157	20	⊜ ⊜ ⊟
Scarborough	158.5	18.5	ⓘ ⌂ ⛺ ⑪ ⊜ ⊕ ⊟ ⊟
Cayton Bay	168.5	8.5	⛺ ⑪
FILEY	177	0	ⓘ ⌂ ⛺ ⑪ ⊜ ⊕ ⊟ ⊟

kms from Filey

ⓘ information centre ⌂ hotel/B&B ⊜ hostel/bunkhouse
⛺ campsite ⑪ café/restaurant ⊕ pub/hotel bar ⊕ shop
⊟ train station ⊟ bus service

One of the steepest parts of the route involves crossing the Rabbit Warren (Yorkshire Wolds Way, Stage 4)

ROUTE SUMMARY TABLE

Stage no	Stage	Stage distance km (miles)	Stage time	Page
The Yorkshire Wolds Way National Trail				
1	Hessle to South Cave	21.5 (13½)	6hr 30min	32
2	South Cave to Goodmanham	18.5 (11½)	5hr 45min or 6hr	40
3	Goodmanham to Millington	15 (9¼)	4hr 45min	47
4	Millington to Thixendale	19.5 (12)	6hr	55
5	Thixendale to Sherburn	30.5 (19)	9hr	61
6	Sherburn to Filey	24 (15)	7hr 30min or 8hr	70
	Total distance	**129 (80¼)**		
7	Filey to Scalby Mills (via the Cleveland Way)	18.5 (11½)	5hr 30min	78
The Tabular Hills Walk				
1	Scalby Mills to Levisham	33.5 (21)	10hr	88
2	Levisham to Hutton-le-Hole	24.5 (15¼)	7hr 30min	96
3	Hutton-le-Hole to Helmsley	22 (13½)	6hr 30min	105
	Total distance	**80 (49¾)**		
The Cleveland Way National Trail				
1	Helmsley to Sutton Bank	17 (10½)	5hr	116
2	Sutton Bank to Osmotherley	19 (11¾)	6hr	121
3	Osmotherley to Clay Bank	17.5 (11)	5hr 15min	126
4	Clay Bank to Kildale	15 (9½)	5hr	133
5	Kildale to Saltburn-by-the-Sea	24 (15)	7hr 30min	139
6	Saltburn-by-the-Sea to Sandsend	27.5 (17)	8hr 30min	148
7	Sandsend to Robin Hood's Bay	16.5 (10¼)	5hr	159
8	Robin Hood's Bay to Scarborough	22 (13¾)	6hr 30min	167
9	Scarborough to Filey	18 (11)	5hr 15min	174
	Total distance	**177 (110)**		
Total for all three trails		**404.5 (251½)**		

The jagged outcrops of the Wain Stones rise in contrast to the gently rolling moors (Cleveland Way, Stage 3)

INTRODUCTION

As a young teenager I pitched my tent for a week near Whitby, safely within sight of the chalet my parents had rented. One evening a man dropped his heavy pack to the ground beside my tent, and I watched in fascination as he sorted out his gear for the night. By the time I woke in the morning he was long gone. He was one of the first Cleveland Way walkers, and I don't know who he was or where he might be now, but I do remember wanting to follow him and see where that long trail went. My parents took me along the cliff path as far as Robin Hood's Bay, but the rest of the route remained a mystery to me for many years.

Eventually I got my chance to walk the Cleveland Way, and I've covered parts of the route many times since. I later walked the Yorkshire Wolds Way, and the Tabular Hills Walk came last of all. I have now had the opportunity to walk all three routes afresh while researching a new edition of this guidebook.

Each of the three routes is described in the guide, and walkers can complete them separately or link all three trails end-to-end in a long-distance walk of over 400km (250 miles). The whole distance could be completed comfortably within three weeks, even allowing for outward travel and return home. Together the three trails open up a wonderfully rich and varied landscape of cultivated countryside, intricate networks of dales, wild heather moorlands and dramatic cliff coastline, peppered with dozens of interesting little towns and villages.

The **Yorkshire Wolds Way** is usually walked from south to north, and extends over 130km (80 miles) from Hessle, near Hull on the Humber Estuary, to Filey. It traverses the Yorkshire Wolds, passing the villages of Welton, Brantingham, South Cave, North Newbald, Goodmanham, Londesborough and Nunburnholme. The central parts of the Wolds are sparsely settled, but the route includes, or passes close to Millington, Huggate, Fridaythorpe, Thixendale, Wharram-le-Street and Wintringham. The northern stretch of the route stays high on the Wolds, but passes Sherburn, Ganton and Muston on the way to Filey. For the sake of a day's march, walkers can continue along the coast to Scarborough and Scalby Mills to join the Tabular Hills Walk.

The **Tabular Hills Walk** takes in the gentle, forested or cultivated southern parts of the North York Moors National Park between Scalby Mills, near Scarborough, and Helmsley, far inland. The route measures 80km (50 miles) and wanders through sparsely settled countryside between Scalby and Levisham, then includes the villages of Newton-on-Rawcliffe, Cropton, Appleton-le-Moors, Hutton-le-Hole, Gillamoor, Fadmoor and Carlton. When the route reaches the bustling market town of Helmsley, walkers can pick up the Cleveland Way and continue along this route back to Filey.

The **Cleveland Way** essentially wraps itself round the North York Moors National Park, covering 177km (110 miles). It traverses the high, western moors and hills at first, where villages are few and far between, passing Rievaulx, Cold Kirby, Sutton Bank, Osmotherley, Carlton Bank, Clay Bank, Kildale, Slapewath and Skelton to reach the coast at Saltburn-by-the-Sea. From that point the route follows the coast and passes a variety of seaside towns and villages. These include Skinningrove, Staithes, Runswick Bay, Kettleness and Sandsend. The busy resort of Whitby is followed by Robin Hood's Bay, Ravenscar and the big, brash resort of Scarborough. All that remains is a day's walk from Scarborough to Filey to bring the Cleveland Way to a close.

Walkers who complete all three trails, whether one at a time or all in one long walk, will cover some of the most attractive, rich and varied countryside in this part of Yorkshire. The gentle landscapes of the Yorkshire Wolds contrast with the bleak and empty moorlands of the North York Moors, and the stark cliff coastline. Quaint little villages contrast with busy market towns and hectic coastal resorts; and always the next waymark and signpost beckon walkers onwards, trekking through Yorkshire's 'broad acres'.

Moorsbus services operate to remote places on summer weekends

PLANNING YOUR TRIP

A pine forest on part of East Heslerton Brow (Yorkshire Wolds Way, Stage 5)

DAILY SCHEDULE

The daily schedule in this guidebook is merely a recommendation, and walkers are of course free to plan their journey along these trails in any way they see fit. It all depends on how far you feel comfortable walking in a day and what your accommodation options are at the end of the day. The route descriptions suggest start and finish points, but also highlight intermediate towns and villages, mentioning if lodgings are available. Everyone has their limit, so if any day's walk seems too long, it is usually possible to split it into shorter stages. Similarly, walkers with good stamina might combine two short stages into one longer day's walk.

WHEN TO WALK

Many walkers probably have an image of the North York Moors that includes purple heather under a blue sky. Such conditions may appear in summer, but bear in mind that the plateau-like nature of the area and its proximity to the sea ensure that misty days are common enough throughout the year. The Yorkshire Wolds, by contrast, feature ploughed fields, green crops and, in early summer, brilliant yellow fields of oilseed rape. Spring can be a wonderful time to walk these routes, when wild flowers are bursting forth and the weather improves day by day, but most walkers opt for the long, bright days of summer. The autumn months can be good, too, with russet hues stealing through the woods and across the bracken slopes.

Winter is for the hardiest of walkers and even the gentle Yorkshire Wolds can be swept by piercingly cold winds. On the higher North York Moors, snow can form drifts that hamper progress just as much as the short daylight hours, and paths along the cliff coast may be dangerous when strong, blustery winds are blowing. A wet winter quickly turns some parts very muddy, although for most of the time the trails follow reasonably firm, dry surfaces that can be used in comfort most of the time. Badly eroded stretches, particularly along the Cleveland Way, were repaired and resurfaced many years ago and now provide a firm footing.

GETTING TO YORKSHIRE

By air
Leeds-Bradford Airport, www.leeds bradfordairport.co.uk, and Manchester Airport, www.manchesterairport. co.uk, are both served by a number of budget airlines from around Europe and have good onward links through Yorkshire. Less useful is Teesside International Airport www.teesside international.com, but it handles flights from Schipol Amsterdam Airport, which is a major European flight hub.

By ferry
Hull is served by P&O Ferries, www. poferries.com, from Rotterdam in the Netherlands and Zeebrugge in Belgium. A simple onward bus or train journey quickly reaches Hessle

Seasonal variations in colour ensure that the landscape constantly changes (Yorkshire Wolds Way, Stage 3)

for the start of the Yorkshire Wolds Way. Alternatively, onward rail or coach journeys can be used to connect with the Cleveland Way and Tabular Hills Walk.

By rail
Hull Trains, www.hulltrains.co.uk, serve Hull from London Kings Cross, with a simple change of train for Hessle and the start of the Yorkshire Wolds Way. There are direct First Transpennine Express, www.tp express.co.uk, trains from Manchester and Leeds to Hull, for the start of the Yorkshire Wolds Way, or to Scarborough, for the Cleveland Way and the start of the Tabular Hills Walk.

By coach
If travelling from Europe, coaches in the Eurolines network, www. eurolines.com, can be linked with those operated by National Express, www.nationalexpress.com, to reach the cities of Hull and Middlesbrough, as well as the coastal resorts of Whitby and Scarborough, on the Cleveland Way, and Filey, at the end of the Yorkshire Wolds Way. Coaches also drop off and pick up at Hessle, at the start of the Yorkshire Wolds Way.

GETTING AROUND YORKSHIRE

Walkers can choose to follow one, two, or all three trails in this guidebook, so there are several possible starting and finishing points. While the start and finish points for all three

trails are well served by public transport, there are places along each trail that lack any kind of public transport.

By train
Northern trains, www.northern railway.co.uk, link Hull, Filey and Scarborough, allowing walkers to reach the beginning and end of the Yorkshire Wolds Way, the beginning of the Tabular Hills Walk and the Cleveland Way. Northern trains also run from Middlesbrough to Kildale and Whitby, linking two parts of the Cleveland Way, and from Middlesbrough to Saltburn, linking with another part of the Cleveland Way. Until the 1960s, there was a coastal railway from Saltburn to Whitby, Robin Hood's Bay and Scarborough. A length of the line serving Skinningrove and Boulby has been preserved for industrial use, while the old trackbed from Whitby to Scarborough has been converted into a footpath and cycleway.

By bus
There are some splendid long-distance bus services through Yorkshire. Yorkshire Coastliner buses, www. transdevbus.co.uk/york, run from Leeds to York, then fan out to reach Filey, for the Yorkshire Wolds Way and Cleveland Way, Scarborough, for the Cleveland Way and Tabular Hills Walk, and Whitby, for the Cleveland Way. With careful attention to routes and timetables, Coastliner buses can be intercepted at Sherburn, on the

Yorkshire Wolds Way, and the Hole of Horcum, on the Tabular Hills Walk.

East Yorkshire buses, www.eastyorkshirebuses.co.uk, link Scarborough and Helmsley, which are both on the Cleveland Way and Tabular Hills Walk. East Yorkshire buses also operate from York to Market Weighton and Hull, crossing the Yorkshire Wolds Way. On summer Sundays and Bank Holidays, the Moors Explorer runs from Hull, serving Wharram Percy on the Yorkshire Wolds Way, continuing across the Tabular Hills Walk at Hutton-le-Hole.

Arriva buses, www.arrivabus.co.uk, operate a long-distance service from Middlesbrough to Guisborough, Whitby, Robin Hood's Bay and Scarborough. They also operate a service from Middlesbrough to Whitby via Saltburn. Apart from the towns, both services also link a number of coastal villages along the Cleveland Way.

There are other minor operators, mentioned where appropriate along the trails, such as Abbots, providing buses linking Osmotherley on the Cleveland Way with Northallerton and Middlesbrough.

The Moorsbus network, www.moorsbus.org, operates on summer weekends, linking inland points of the Tabular Hills Walk and the Cleveland Way that other bus services don't reach.

Traveline
Walkers who need specific information about public transport links can call Traveline, tel 0871 2002233, www.traveline.info. Always try to anticipate your transport needs and check timetables in advance, rather than leaving everything to the last minute. There is little point in reaching a bus stop 10 minutes late, with no more buses until the next day.

ACCOMMODATION

There are specific accommodation lists for the Cleveland Way and Yorkshire Wolds Way, listing plenty of hotels, guesthouses, bed-and-breakfasts, youth hostels, camping barns and campsites that might easily be overlooked, especially if they lie a little off-route. However, bear in mind that accommodation inland tends to be rather limited in some places. These accommodation lists do not carry full details of the hundreds of addresses that are available in the popular resorts, but contact the tourist information centres, who can offer suggestions. Finding somewhere to stay along the Tabular Hills Walk needs careful thought, as places are unevenly spaced and some of the villages have no accommodation to offer.

Many accommodation options can be checked, booked and paid for using online services such as www.airbnb.com and www.booking.com. These sites allow walkers to see where properties are located in relation to the trails, and they also show which properties are available at short notice.

All services in Huggate revolve around the Wolds Inn (Yorkshire Wolds Way, Stage 4)

Two guides, the *Cleveland Way Accommodation and Information Guide* and the *Yorkshire Wolds Way Accommodation and Information Guide,* can be obtained from the North York Moors National Park Authority, The Old Vicarage, Helmsley, York, YO62 5BP, tel 01439 770657. These lists can also be checked online, or downloaded and printed from www.nationaltrail.co.uk/cleveland-way and www.nationaltrail.co.uk/yorkshire-wolds-way.

Please bear in mind that once you make a booking with an accommodation provider a contract exists between you. If you fail to show they may be entitled to keep any deposit you have paid, or even the whole sum if they are unable to let your room to anyone else. If you change your plans or know you are going to be late, phone and let them know as soon as possible. It could happen that your accommodation provider thinks you are lost and may worry sufficiently to alert the emergency services!

TOURIST INFORMATION CENTRES

Many towns and some villages along these trails have tourist information centres and these are mentioned at the relevant points in the route descriptions, so use them as the best source of local accommodation information. The larger centres may be willing to book lodgings on your behalf for a nominal fee, and they will also have details of local attractions and events, as well as timetables for local bus and rail services. Larger centres usually have detailed town plans, Ordnance Survey maps, guidebooks, and local crafts and souvenirs for sale. A selection of tourist information centres lying reasonably close to each of the trails can be found in Appendix A.

Information websites

An excellent all-round website covering the North York Moors National Park is www.northyorkmoors.org. uk. A good online resource for the Yorkshire Wolds is www.visit hullandeastyorkshire.com. The official website for the Cleveland Way is www.nationaltrail.co.uk/cleveland-way. The official website for the Yorkshire Wolds Way is www.national trail.co.uk/yorkshire-wolds-way. The Long Distance Walkers Association, www.ldwa.org.uk, offers plenty of information about the trails in this guidebook, and links to all types of accommodation along them.

or cafés will be open when you reach them. It can be galling to walk for hours, working up a thirst, to find the village pub is closed, so always ensure that some food and drink is carried during the day.

Some accommodation providers offer meals, but may require advance notice, and similarly they may offer packed lunches if notified at least the evening before. Places that do not offer food may be able to recommend somewhere nearby, and in remote locations they might be willing to drive walkers to and from pubs or restaurants, but check if lifts are available when making bookings.

FOOD AND DRINK

The coastal resorts abound with a choice of food and drink that can be really quite bewildering at times, although the staple fish and chips rules supreme and the smell of deep-fat frying can be overwhelming! Further inland, both on the North York Moors and Yorkshire Wolds, the choice may be much more limited, and indeed there may be times when nothing is available all day long. Places where refreshments may be available are mentioned in each day's route description, although there is no guarantee that pubs, restaurants

MONEY

While an increasing number of accommodation providers, shops, pubs and restaurants will take credit cards in payment, many don't, and walkers will need a certain amount of cash for goods and services while on the move, especially on the more remote parts of these trails. If unsure about carrying large amounts of cash, at least try and budget ahead, then be aware of any places along the way that have banks and ATMs. Many are mentioned in the route descriptions, and some supermarkets offer a cash-back service.

PLANNING DAY BY DAY

The celebrated whalebone arch on the way down to Whitby harbour (Cleveland Way, Stage 7)

USING THIS GUIDE

An information box at the beginning of each stage provides the essential facts for the day's walk: start and finish points (including grid refs), distance covered, an overview of the types of terrain you'll encounter, relevant OS Landranger and Explorer sheets, places en route (as well as slightly off-route) where you can buy refreshments, and details of public transport.

Stage maps, extracted from the Ordnance Survey mapping, are provided at a scale of 1:50,000. In the route description, significant places or features along the way that also appear on the map extracts are highlighted in **bold** to aid navigation. As

well as the route being described in detail, background information about places of interest is provided in brief.

Appendix A provides contact details that may be useful in planning and enjoying a successful walk.

MAPS OF THE ROUTES

This guidebook contains extracts from Ordnance Survey Landranger mapping at a scale of 1:50,000, with a clear route overlay. These are perfectly adequate for following any of the trails described. The map booklet shows the whole route of the Cleveland Way on 1:25,000 mapping. To appreciate the surrounding countryside to

Erosion problems on popular parts of trails have been completely eradicated (Cleveland Way, Stage 3)

a greater extent, carry some or all of the following maps: Ordnance Survey 1:50,000 Landranger sheets 93, 94, 99, 100, 101 and 106. For greater detail use the Ordnance Survey 1:25,000 Explorer sheets OL26, OL27, 293, 294, 300 and 301. The appropriate Landranger and Explorer maps for each day along these trails are shown in the information box at the start of each day's route description. For further details visit www. ordnancesurvey.co.uk. Harvey Maps produce a 1:40,000 scale National Trail map of the Cleveland Way, www.harveymaps.co.uk.

Ordnance Survey and Harvey Maps are available in digital form for those who wish to navigate using a GPS or an app used on a GPS-enabled device.

WAYMARKING

Waymarks for the Yorkshire Wolds Way and the Cleveland Way are the standard national trail acorn logo, along with directional arrows. Signposts may simply read 'Wolds Way' or 'Cleveland Way', or they may also include one of the next destinations along the trail. Signposts and waymarks for the Tabular Hills Walk feature a directional arrow and a 'Tabular Hills' logo.

RESCUE SERVICES

In the unlikely event that emergency assistance is needed, simply dial 999 (or the European emergency number 112). State clearly whether you need the police, ambulance, fire service, mountain rescue or coastguard, and be ready to give full details of the emergency. Ensure that you give your phone number so that the emergency services can keep in touch. Members of the public cannot request direct helicopter assistance – their call-out and use will be determined by the emergency services, based on the information you provide. As these trails often wander through remote countryside, a small first-aid kit should be carried to deal with any minor cuts, grazes and other injuries along the way. Aim to be self-sufficient each day by carrying appropriate food and drink in your pack.

TRAIL OFFICER

If any problems are noticed on any of the trails in this guidebook, please note full details and contact: National Trail Officer, North York Moors National Park, The Old Vicarage, Bondgate, Helmsley, YO62 5BP, tel 01439 772700.

ALL ABOUT THE NORTH YORK MOORS AND THE YORKSHIRE WOLDS

Telltale bare slopes, left by the alum industry at Kettleness (Cleveland Way, Stage 6)

BRIEF HISTORY

Around 10,000BC, during Mesolithic times, nomadic hunter-gatherers found a much different landscape than today's visitors do. The Yorkshire Wolds and North York Moors were largely wooded, with cliff coastlines facing the North Sea. Inland, vast marshlands were subject to seasonal flooding, so that between the mouth of the River Tees and the Humber Estuary, the upland parts of East Yorkshire was almost an island, offering the only firm footing for settlers. Flint tools are basically all that remind us of this period of occupation. In Neolithic times, about 3000BC, the land began to be cleared and cultivated, especially in the Yorkshire Wolds and Tabular Hills where the soil was more fertile. People were settled in communities and were sufficiently organised to be able to construct burial mounds and earthworks. By 1900BC Bronze Age invaders had arrived in the area and their settlements were more defensive. These people continued to develop agriculture, but due to climatic changes were forced to abandon the higher parts of the North York Moors, which reverted to heath and tree scrub. Iron Age invaders came into the area around 300BC, followed by the Romans from 71AD. With the Romans came roads, forts and efficient communications, with signal stations constructed along the east coast. The Angles and Danes put the Romans under pressure from the fifth century, when the Roman Empire was beginning to fall apart.

Anglo-Saxon methods of cultivation were based around open field systems near villages. When the Normans pushed into the area in the 11th century the infamous 'harrying of the north' left many people as refugees on their own land, unable to call anywhere home or grow crops or rear livestock. Land was parcelled out among the conquerors. Fine abbeys and monasteries were founded, as well as stout stone castles. The Black Death of the 14th century left the landscape littered with abandoned villages, particularly in the Yorkshire Wolds. The Wolds became a great sheep-rearing area and an immensely important producer of wool.

In the 16th century the North York Moors became a large-scale producer of alum (a valuable salt used as a fixative in the dyeing process) and vast areas of land became part of what was in effect a huge, early chemical industry that spanned two-and-a-half centuries. Alum quarrying was mainly located along the coast and the cliff edges of the Cleveland Hills, the interior being largely a wasteland crisscrossed by trading routes where no one was inclined to linger for long. To aid travellers across the moors, stone waymark crosses were planted. Settlement remained confined to the dales, with the moors bleak and barren. Just as alum production drew to a close, ironstone production reached its peak.

The 18th century saw the Yorkshire Wolds switch from sheep rearing to intensive agriculture, with the higher ground divided into huge, square fields planted with cereals.

JET

Jet, often known as 'Whitby jet', has been used to create ornaments and jewellery since the Bronze Age. It is found in certain beds of rock that outcrop around the North York Moors, often along the coast, but also far inland around Carlton Bank. Basically, jet is nothing more than a type of coal, but it is distinctive because it was formed from isolated logs of driftwood, rather than the thick masses of decayed vegetation that form regular coal seams. High-quality jet is tough and black, can be turned on a lathe or carved, and takes a high polish. Jet has been used to create everything from intricately carved statuettes to shiny beads and facetted stones for jewellery. Jet crafting has long centred on Whitby, with production peaking in the 19th century. See www.whitbyjet.co.uk.

ALUM

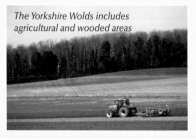

The Yorkshire Wolds includes agricultural and wooded areas

Throughout the North York Moors National Park walkers encounter huge piles of flaky pink shale dumped on the landscape, sometimes along the western fringes of the Cleveland Hills, but more especially along the coast. These are the remains of a large-scale chemical industry that thrived from 1600 to 1870. The hard-won prize was alum, a valuable salt that could be extracted from certain beds of shale by a tortuous and time-consuming process.

Wherever the shale occurred it was extensively quarried. Millions of tons were cut, changing the shape of the landscape considerably, especially along the coast. Wood, and in later years coal, was mixed in layers with the broken shale, and great piles like small hills were fired and kept burning for months – or even for a whole year. Burnt shale was put into huge tanks of water to soak – a process known as leaching – then the water was drawn off and boiled, which required more wood and coal, as well as treatment with such odious substances as human urine, brought to the area from as far away as London. As crystals of precious alum began to form, the process ended with a purification stage before the end product was packed for dispatch.

Alum had many uses, but was chiefly in demand as a fixative for dyes, allowing cloth to be strongly coloured and colour-fast after washing. The Italians had a virtual monopoly on alum production until the alum shale of Yorkshire was exploited from 1600. The local industry went into a sudden decline when other sources of alum and more advanced dyeing methods were discovered from 1850. The long and involved process of quarrying, burning, leaching, boiling, crystallisation and purification was replaced by simpler, cheaper and faster means of production.

The main alum-producing sites along the course of the Cleveland Way are evident around Carlton Bank, Slapewath, Boulby Cliff, Kettleness, Sandsend, Saltwick Bay and Ravenscar. Another two dozen sites are scattered off-route across the landscape. Look on these stark remains, consider the toil and labour, and bear in mind that it all took place so that fine gentlemen and ladies could wear brightly coloured clothes!

IRONSTONE

Cleveland ironstone was mined and quarried from around 500BC, as evidenced by an ancient bloomery site on Levisham Moor (a 'bloomery' was where malleable iron was produced directly by burning iron ore). However, large-scale working didn't commence until around 1850, when moorland and coastal locations such as Skinningrove and Rosedale were exploited. The tiny coastal village of Skinningrove became known as 'the valley of iron' as a major steelworks was developed. Ironstone from Rosedale was transported over the moors by rail to be loaded into blast furnaces at Middlesbrough. Huge quantities of coal had to be shipped to the area, while industry and commerce was hungry for the iron that was produced. The last local ironstone mine, at North Skelton, closed in 1964. Steelworks at Middlesbrough are now much reduced, while Skinningrove only just manages to remain in production.

The Tabular Hills were cultivated in similar fashion, although the broader North York Moors began to be managed more for sport, with grouse shooting pre-eminent. Scrub was cleared and vast areas were selectively burnt to encourage the growth of heather, providing suitable cover and feeding for grouse, to the delight of 19th-century sportsmen. In the 20th century moorland began to be ploughed and planted, or 'improved' as pasture for grazing sheep and cattle, but following the establishment of the North York Moors National Park in 1952, the process was curtailed.

WOLDS, MOORS AND COAST

There are three essential elements to the landscapes traversed in this guidebook. The Yorkshire Wolds are chalk uplands of no great height, intensively cultivated, with the appearance of an enormous patchwork quilt, but dissected by attractive grassy and wooded valleys, sprinkled with charming villages and farming hamlets. These uplands are explored by following the Yorkshire Wolds Way.

The North York Moors National Park is broad and undulating, flushed purple each summer, but bleak and wild when swept by winter gales. Stout stone villages nestle deep in the dales. The moors are explored using the Tabular Hills Walk in the south, as well as the huge loop of the Cleveland Way. Space and solitude characterise these moors, and while many walkers believe it is a wild landscape, the expanse of heather is in fact entirely man-managed to provide a favourable habitat for grouse. Extensive areas have also been planted with forests, although 'improvement' of moorland

Much of the cliff coastline is designated 'heritage coast' and abounds in interest (Cleveland Way, Stage 6)

to create more farmland was largely brought to a halt when the North York Moors National Park was established in 1952.

The crumbling cliff coast is the third element, rising high above the North Sea, but cut by river valleys where fishing ports have turned their attention to tourism. The coastline from Saltburn-by-the-Sea to Scalby has been designated 'heritage coast' on account of its rich historical interest. The coastal Cleveland Way passes the start of the Tabular Hills Walk and also joins directly with the Yorkshire Wolds Way. Despite being of relatively low stature, never rising above 454m (1490ft), the uplands traversed in this guidebook feature several ascents and descents, some of which can be quite steep. Overall there is great variety and interest for wayfarers who attempt any or all of these trails, but Yorkshire is a huge area and this guidebook only covers one corner of it.

THE YORKSHIRE WOLDS WAY NATIONAL TRAIL

A windmill tower is passed on the way out of Hessle (Stage 1)

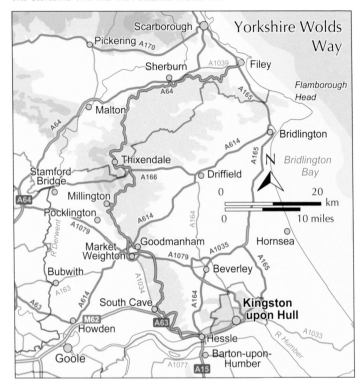

The Yorkshire Wolds rise lush and green from the muddy brown shore of the Humber Estuary, and roll gently northwards before falling abruptly into the North Sea between Filey and Bridlington. The Wolds are merely the northernmost extent of a broad band of chalk that stretches the length of England to Kent and Dorset. The chalk appears as sheer cliffs at Flamborough Head, but inland it forms a gently sloping tableland. This is covered by a huge patchwork quilt of intensively cultivated fields cut by a maze of steep-sided grassy dales, the latter used for grazing sheep and occasionally cattle or horses. The landscape is sparsely dotted with small villages and widely spaced farms – water was always in short supply, making it difficult to support large towns.

The bedrock of the Yorkshire Wolds is porous chalk, laid down in the Cretaceous period some 70 to 100 million years ago. Although the land does not readily support flowing water, glacial melt-water flowed vigorously after the Ice Age and cut many valleys deep into the landscape. Flint occurs as nodules in beds of chalk and is easily spotted whenever the land is ploughed. The first settlers used flint for sharp-edged scrapers, blades and arrowheads. Several ancient settlement sites occur on the Wolds, along with burial mounds and as yet unexplained earthworks. There are also deserted village sites, either abandoned during the Black Death of the 14th century or fallen idle due to changes in agricultural practices. The Wolds are fertile, but as the soil is relatively thin and dry, it is mostly planted with grain and oilseed rape rather than root crops, and colours change throughout the seasons. Towns are found on the lower ground, away from the uplands, where water was more easily obtained.

Local members of the Ramblers' Association first suggested back in 1969 that a Wolds Way should be established, and in the same year East Riding County Council agreed that such a route should exist. The route had gained approval by 1971, but it wasn't until 1982 that it was finally declared open. Despite gaining National Trail status the Wolds Way has always been one of the quietest of Britain's long-distance walking routes. The scenery is charming and interesting, but it lacks the drama of high mountains, open moorlands, sheer cliffs and wilderness. In 2004 the route was renamed the Yorkshire Wolds Way with the intention of relaunching it in the public awareness. While it would be no bad thing for more walkers to experience and appreciate the route, as well as the wider Yorkshire Wolds, it has to be said that facilities such as accommodation, food and drink are sparse or absent over long stretches. However, such problems can be overcome with careful planning and the route can be enjoyed with relative ease.

Waymarks for the route are the standard national trail acorn logo, along with directional arrows. Stout wooden posts are passed every 8km (5 miles). Signposts may simply read 'Wolds Way', or they may also include one of the next destinations along the trail. The entire trail was declared completely free of stiles in 2015. Keep up to date with developments and diversions by checking the website www.national trail.co.uk/yorkshire-wolds-way, and obtain or download a current copy of the *Yorkshire Wolds Way Accommodation and Information Guide*.

STAGE 1
Hessle to South Cave

Start	Railway station, Hessle (TA 029 256)
Finish	Jubilee Clock, South Cave (SE 923 313)
Distance	21.5km (13½ miles)
Time	6hr 30min
Terrain	Easy roads, tracks and paths along the coast, but one stretch is covered at high water, requiring a detour inland. The route runs through woods, giving way to fields later.
Maps	OS Landranger 106, OS Explorer 293
Refreshments	Pubs off-route in Hessle. Pub restaurant near the Humber Bridge. Pubs off-route at Ferriby. Pub restaurant at Welton. Plenty of choice at South Cave.
Public transport	Buses and trains run regularly between Hull, Hessle and North Ferriby. East Yorkshire buses regularly link Hull, Hessle, North Ferriby, Welton, Brantingham and South Cave with Market Weighton and York.

The Yorkshire Wolds Way starts on a low-key note in Hessle, almost as if it has lost its way before even going anywhere. However, things quickly become more scenic and interesting as the route progresses along the coast. There is a choice of routes at North Ferriby – a muddy low-tide beach walk or a high-tide road-walk inland. There are well-wooded areas on the way to and from the village of Welton, while open, cultivated countryside interspersed with more wooded areas occurs later. Slopes are fairly gentle for the most part. Villages lie just off-route during this day's walk, so short detours are required in order to admire their cosy cottages and fine old houses. Both Welton and Brantingham have pubs, while South Cave has more places offering food and drink.

Those who arrive in the evening can turn right to find a guest house.

Start at the railway station at **Hessle**, cross a footbridge over the busy **A63** road and turn left along Livingstone Road. ◄ The former Ferryboat Inn stands on a corner, where a right turn reveals the first Yorkshire Wolds Way signpost, as well as signs for the Transpennine Trail. A short path, Jean's Walk, leads quickly to the estuary of the **River Humber**, into which one-fifth of England's rivers drain. The tarmac path runs to a small car park where a stone sculpture commemorates the Wolds Way. Study the place-names carved deep into the stone, as these will become familiar during the week ahead. Walk along a grassy strip between the coast and a road to reach the graceful span of the **Humber Bridge**. Marvel at its size and architecture while passing one of its towering supports embedded deep in the ground.

The graceful span of the Humber Bridge, looking from Lincolnshire to Yorkshire

A tunnel and railway bridge had been proposed long before the current **road bridge over the Humber** was approved. Opened in 1981, it was at the time the longest single-span bridge in the world. The length of road between the two supports is 2.2km (1.4 miles) and the cost of construction was £91 million. There is a special viewing area and visitor centre offering full details of the structure.

Pass a windmill stump – the Hessle Whiting Mill – and keep seawards of the Country Park Inn, or pass inland if the tide is in. Come ashore and follow a clear track along a narrow strip of land between the muddy shore and a busy railway line. Buddleia and brambles are tangled together alongside. Later, the Riverside Walkway runs the through a pleasant and grassy area, passing a point where the remains of a Bronze Age boat were discovered. A representation of its shape is set into the ground. Approaching **North Ferriby**, a decision needs to be made about which of two routes to take, depending on the state of the tide.

If the tide is out or the water is unlikely to cover the beach in the

map continues on page 37

next half hour, then go down concrete steps and walk along the beach. Avoid muddy patches and slippery boulders, and bear in mind that most of the landward bank is private for the next 750m (800 yards). However, another flight of concrete steps offers access inland in case of difficulty. Continue along the shore to climb a flight of metal steps. Turn left, then turn right inland along a clear woodland track through **Long Plantation**. This later crosses a bridge over a railway line and reaches the busy **A63** road.

High-water route

If the tide is in, then head inland past the Reed Pond and turn left along Ings Lane. Turn right along Humber Road and walk straight ahead to cross a footbridge over the railway line at **Ferriby** railway station. Continue straight ahead along Station Road and Narrow Lane, which indeed becomes very narrow. Turn left along High Street and keep following it to continue along Melton Road. Keep left to walk alongside the busy **A63** road.

With both routes reunited, the main road is too dangerous to cross, so walk as signposted up to a roundabout. Use a pedestrian crossing, then cross a bridge to reach another roundabout. A tarmac path is signposted alongside a slip road. Follow it, then turn left up a path to cross the well-wooded **Melton Hill**. Cross a track to reach the North Hull Scout Campsite. ▸

Follow a track down through the campsite to reach another busy road. Cross with care, then follow a broad and clear track straight uphill

A stout and distinctive 5-mile marker post is passed. Others will be passed every 5 miles (8 kilometres), all the way to Filey.

alongside a **quarry** fence. The 'Omya' quarry extracts chalk purely as a source of calcium carbonate, as a paint filler and for chemical industries. Note that blasting can take place any time between 0800 and 1630, Monday to Friday.

Walk up the track until a Wolds Way signpost points left along a wooded path. This quickly turns right to continue alongside the edge of the woodland, overlooking fields. The path later drifts into the wood and reaches a junction of tracks. Turn left along a rather battered road called Chapel Hill, which improves as it descends to a small green at **Welton**. The Wolds Way turns right along Dale Road, but walkers may wish to go straight ahead into the village first, for food and drink.

> The fine little village of **Welton** has a canal-like stream running through it, so that St Helen's Church looks as though it is marooned on an island. The 17th-century Green Dragon Inn offers food, drink and accommodation. This is where the notorious highwayman Dick Turpin was arrested in 1739. East Yorkshire buses link Welton with South Cave, North Ferriby, Hessle and Hull.

Follow Dale Road out of Welton, passing a couple of millponds. The road becomes a track leading to a solitary cottage. Pass a gate and walk through the half-wooded and half-grassy floor of **Welton Dale**, which becomes more wooded after passing another gate. Follow the most obvious path up to a concrete access road, and cross over it. Turn right to follow a path parallel to the road, then turn left as signposted for the Wolds Way. The path has a forest on the left and open fields on the right, and runs directly north to pass a pond that might not even be noticed. Turn left along a track, then almost immediately right to walk away from buildings at **Wauldby Manor Farm**.

A clear track runs through fields, passes a big beech tree, then drops to an intersection of tracks. Turn left as signposted Wolds Way and follow a path up through a shelter belt of woodland. Emerge at a road junction and

simply walk straight ahead along Elloughton Dale Road until the road suddenly turns left. At this point walk straight ahead along a clear track, which is later blocked against traffic by tree trunks.

A clear track passes fields near Wauldby Manor Farm

The grassy track leads gently uphill beside **Long Plantation**, over 140m (460ft) on **Brantingham Wold**. Pass another tree-trunk barrier and a 5-mile marker post, to continue straight ahead along a minor road that soon begins to drop steeply towards

map continues on page 39

Brantingham. The village is off-route but the road

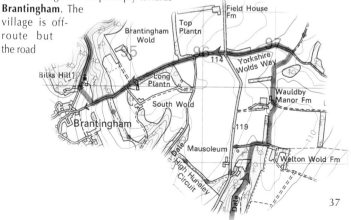

37

A grassy track runs beside Long Plantation, over Brantingham Wold to Brantingham

leads straight there if desired, otherwise turn right through a kissing gate signposted for the Wolds Way. Walk down a steep path, fenced on both sides, then turn right towards All Saints Church on Dale Road.

> Facilities in the fine old estate village of **Brantingham** are quite limited and it is necessary to walk all the way to the far side to find them. The Triton Inn serves food and drink, and there is a bus shelter opposite. East Yorkshire buses link Brantingham with South Cave, Welton, North Ferriby, Hessle and Hull.

Note the Cattle Well on the right of Dale Road, just inside the grounds of the Old Stables.

Follow Dale Road up through the wooded valley. ◀ Pass the Sheep Wash and later turn left up a clear track. A path runs parallel to the track, crossing a gap between two small hills on **Ellerker North Wold**. Walk straight down a sunken path flanked by wire fences towards **Woodale Farm**, then turn right to follow a track as signposted. Later, turn left off the track and cross a small wooded dale, then climb a steep, grassy slope. Go through a kissing gate and walk beside a wood. Go through another kissing gate and soon pass through a shelter belt of woodland to walk alongside a field near **Mount Airy Farm**, at 130m (425ft), to reach a track.

Turn left along the track and walk down the farm access road, turning right to pass quickly through a belt of woodland. The road crosses a large field then turns left to drop steeply down to a lower road. ▶ Turn left to walk towards **South Cave**. The village centre is actually off-route, and just as its outskirts are reached the Wolds Way is signposted off to the right. However, most walkers will be happy to visit and maybe stay overnight in the village.

It is actually called Steep Hill!

SOUTH CAVE

Dominated by its Jubilee Clock, South Cave is a busy little village offering a good range of facilities. The Fox & Coney offers food, drink and lodgings and The Bear is another pub serving food and drink. There is also a restaurant, café, take-away, a bank with an ATM, a post office and a few shops. The Cave Castle Hotel offers luxury accommodation. East Yorkshire buses regularly link South Cave with Hull, Hessle, North Ferriby, Brantingham, Market Weighton and York, although some run more directly to and from Hull.

STAGE 2

*South Cave to Goodmanham or
Market Weighton*

Start	Jubilee Clock, South Cave (SE 923 313)
Finish	Goodmanham Parish Church (SE 890 432), or
	Londesborough Arms, Market Weighton (SE 877 417)
Distance	18.5 or 19.5km (11½ or 12 miles)
Time	5hr 45min or 6hr
Terrain	Easy roads, tracks and paths with a few ascents and
	descents on reasonably gentle slopes. Route-finding is
	intricate at first but easier later.
Maps	OS Landranger 106, OS Explorer 293
Refreshments	Pubs off-route in North Newbald. Pub and tearoom at
	Goodmanham. Plenty of choice at Market Weighton.
Public transport	East Yorkshire buses regularly link Hull, South Cave
	and Market Weighton with Pocklington and York. Other
	services operate via Beverley, crossing the Wolds Way at
	Arras, offering a link with Market Weighton.

The Yorkshire Wolds increase in height as this day's walk unfolds, although the higher parts are simply rolling fields rather than hills. A series of charming, steep-sided dales are visited – some wooded, some grassy – two of which have had railways routed through them in the past. After leaving South Cave facilities actually on the route are very limited indeed. North Newbald lies 1.5km (1 mile) off-route if food and drink are required in the middle of the day. The remote farmstead of Arras lies near a regular bus route. Once beyond it, walkers are faced with a choice of routes. Either follow the main route to Goodmanham, which has a pub and bed-and-breakfast, or take an alternative loop through Market Weighton, where there are several opportunities to enjoy food and drink and there are regular bus services.

Leave **South Cave** by following Beverley Road out of the village, then turn left after the last house, as signposted for the Wolds Way. Cross a footbridge and follow a narrow path uphill beside a small plantation of willow. Walk into **Little Wold Plantation** and turn right to follow a broad woodland path. ▶ The path climbs almost to 120m (395ft) to reach a junction with a wider track. Turn right to walk down the track, which is flanked by trees and bushes but allows a glimpse back to the Humber Estuary. Watch out for a kissing gate on the left where the Wolds Way runs down a grassy path through the little Comber Dale. Swing right near the bottom of the slope, overlooking a wooded hollow containing springs, to reach a bridle kissing gate – a huge kissing gate for horses.

The wood is managed by the Woodland Trust and enjoys open access.

Cross over an old railway trackbed in **Weedley Dale**. This railway ran from 1885 to 1959. Don't follow the trackbed, but turn right as marked to follow a woodland track above the cutting. Later, join another track and turn right and left as marked through the well-wooded **East Dale**. Later, fork left at a signposted junction and the track narrows as it climbs. Emerge from the woods into a field and turn left to walk round the edge, passing a 5-mile marker post to reach the busy B1230. Cross with care, go into a field and turn right to walk parallel to the road to High Hunsley Beacon, at 162m (532ft). The beacon was erected by Rowley Parish Council in 2002. (Hunsley Beacon is also the name of a prominent nearby transmitter mast.)

Turn left to walk alongside a field, then turn right along a quiet road and head straight through a crossroads, from Whin

map continues on page 43

41

Following a grassy path through a large ploughed field in Swin Dale

Lane onto Littlewood Road. Follow the road alongside a strip of woodland called North Plantation. Turn left alongside another field, keeping right of a hedge, and turn right around a corner of the field. Go through a small gate and drop into a dale, turning left through an old gateway, which is no more than a stout post in a gap in an old hedge. Walk down through the dale, where the steep slopes are used for sheep grazing. Turn left at a Wolds Way signpost to reach a confluence of dales and continue down through Swin Dale.

Follow the path as marked through gates, and it becomes a clear grassy track further down through the dale. The floor of the dale is cultivated, while its steep slopes remain untilled, with a fringe of trees along its upper brow. When a minor road is reached the Wolds Way turns right, but walkers who need food and drink can turn left and walk off-route to North Newbald.

The village of **North Newbald** is 1.5km (1 mile) off-route, offering a few facilities in an area otherwise lacking services. Facing each other beside The Green are two pubs, The Gnu Inn and the Tiger

Inn, both serving food and drink and the former also providing accommodation. Bus services run back to South Cave, North Ferriby and Hull, and ahead to Market Weighton and York. Use Eastgate, the road signposted for Beverley, to get back onto the Wolds Way. East Yorkshire buses regularly link North Newbald with Hull, South Cave, Market Weighton, Pocklington and York.

Follow the road past a farm and turn left up a clear track to reach a higher road on **Newbald Wold**. Turn right along this road, then left up another broad, clear track. When the track levels out it passes a trig point at 144m (472ft) and there are good views around the higher parts of the Wolds, although a clutch of nearby wind turbines is rather distracting. The track

map continues on page 45

43

The Wolds Way uses a high track between Newbald Wold and Hessleskew

passes under a pylon line and passes a 5-mile marker post near **Hessleskew Gare**.

The route continues along a track beside a large field and reaches a minor road. ◄ Walk straight ahead along the road, rising slightly to pass a farm and a few houses in a clump of trees at **Hessleskew**. Keep walking along and gently down the road to reach a junction with the busy A1079. Buses pass regularly, but be sure to give a clear hand signal to stop one.

Cross the busy main road with care and fork left along the farm access road, whose tree-lined avenue leads to the farmstead of **Arras** in a small woodland at over 120m (395ft). Simply walk straight through the farmyard and turn left to continue. The Wolds Way runs alongside enormous fields, initially tracing an overhead power line away from the farm across Weighton Wold. A grassy track later runs down a slope to reach a gate at a road junction. Walk straight ahead to follow a minor road down to an intersection with an old railway trackbed, now signposted as the Hudson Way, where a decision needs to be made about a choice of routes.

The main route continues to Goodmanham, but lacks all but the most basic facilities. The alternative route goes

The village of Sancton is almost 3km (2 miles) away, offering a pub and bus services.

to Market Weighton today, which offers more in the way of services, for the sake of an extra 1km (½ mile). Both routes re-join early on Stage 3 in Londesborough Park.

For the main route, simply stay on the road to follow the main course of the Wolds Way. The road climbs out of the wooded dale, swinging right to proceed at a gentler gradient. Turn left at a road junction to walk down into **Goodmanham**.

> The delightful little village of **Goodmanham** surrounds an old church and features fine houses and cottages. Of particular note in the church is the lavish baptismal font carved with the words, 'wyth owt baptysm no soull ma be saved'. The only facilities are the Goodmanham Arms, Fiddle Drill tearoom and a campsite at Manor Farm. Jubilee House offers accommodation, halfway down the road to Market Weighton.

Alternative route for Market Weighton

Turn left along the old railway trackbed, which is signposted as the Hudson Way. ▶ Follow the track through a well-wooded dale, passing St Helen's Well. There is no doubting the way ahead, which is always clear and generally flanked by trees and bushes. The route soon brushes alongside **Market Weighton**. Pass a children's play park, then turn left to enter town by way of Station Road and a passage beside All Saints Church, known as Church Side. This

The line operated from 1865 to 1965 and its founder, George Hudson, made and lost a fortune on the enterprise.

45

The alternative route follows the Hudson Way railway path into Market Weighton

leads to High Street beside the Londesborough Arms, where plenty of shops are in view.

MARKET WEIGHTON

Market Weighton is the only town of any size actually on the Wolds Way, apart from Filey at the end, and it offers a good range of services. While considering its size, also consider the size of William Bradley, born at Bradley House on York Road in 1792, and buried in the churchyard of All Saints Church in 1820. He was the tallest man in the country, standing 2.36m (7ft 9ins). A life-size statue stands near his birthplace.

The only place offering accommodation actually in the town is the Londesborough Arms but there are places in the surrounding countryside. There are banks with ATMs, a post office, toilets, plenty of pubs, restaurants, cafés and takeaways, as well as a range of shops. East Yorkshire buses regularly link Market Weighton with Hull, Beverley, South Cave, Pocklington and York.

STAGE 3

Goodmanham or Market Weighton to Millington

Start	Goodmanham Parish Church (SE 890 432), or Londesborough Arms, Market Weighton (SE 877 417)
Finish	Ramblers Rest, Millington (SE 831 518)
Distance	15 or 15.5km (9¼ or 9½ miles)
Time	4hr 45min
Terrain	Mostly low-level walking along quiet roads, tracks and field paths, ending with a steep descent.
Maps	OS Landranger 106, OS Explorer 294
Refreshments	Pub at the end of the day in Millington. Café off-route at Kilnwick Percy. Pubs, restaurants, cafés and takeaways off-route in Pocklington.
Public transport	East Yorkshire buses regularly link Market Weighton with South Cave, Beverley, Hull, Pocklington and York. Tuesday-only buses link Pocklington with Nunburnholme and Huggate.

The Wolds Way was split at the end of the previous day's route description, with walkers on the main route going to Goodmanham and those on the alternative route going to Market Weighton. Both routes combine fairly early in Londesborough Park. The day's walk to Millington is through undemanding countryside with no significant ascents or descents until the end of the day. While facilities are scarce during the day there are opportunities to detour off-route to the market town of Pocklington if a greater range of services are required. There might also be time to include a diversion to Kilnwick Percy Hall, now run as a Buddhist centre. Beyond Millington the Wolds Way features some strenuous ascents and descents, so walkers might appreciate a leisurely day first.

For those on the main route, leave **Goodmanham** by following the Wolds Way as signposted at the top end

Goodmanham's fine old stone church is on the main Wolds Way

of the churchyard. The route leaves the village and runs straight down a track and under an old railway bridge. Continue onwards, swinging left to follow a broad grassy strip between large fields and hedges. Turn right in the corner of a field to head straight for the busy A163 road at the **Towthorpe Corner** picnic site. Cross the main road to continue.

The Wolds Way runs straight ahead through fields, continuing onwards using a farm access road. Watch for a gate on the left where a grassy slope leads gently down to another gate. Cross a footbridge between a small pond and **The Lake**, where waterfowl can be spotted, which is a rare opportunity in the largely waterless Wolds. Note a stout 5-mile marker post, then walk uphill and follow a grassy track, turning left as marked along another track to go through a gate. The track continues through **Londesborough Park**, a pleasant, grassy area dotted with fine trees. The main route reaches a junction with the alternative route at a three-fingered Yorkshire Wolds Way signpost where a right turn leads up to **Londesborough**.

Alternative start from Market Weighton

Leave by following York Road out of town. Just as the outskirts are reached turn right as signposted straight across a field. The Wolds Way continues alongside fields, crossing small footbridges over a handful of field drains. These lower fields have deeper, finer soil than the high Wolds, and so can be used for root crops as well as grain and oilseed rape. A grassy track leads to the busy A163, which wayfarers simply cross to continue along a farm access road. This leads to **Towthorpe Grange**.

Walk onwards as marked and cross over **Towthorpe Beck**. The route runs through or alongside fields and generally parallel to the beck, although this is often unseen. A grassy track leads to a minor road where you turn left and then right to go through a monumental gate at a gate house. Follow a track straight ahead into

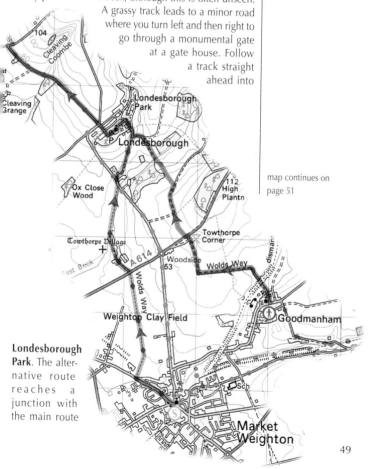

map continues on page 51

Londesborough Park. The alternative route reaches a junction with the main route

49

A fine little pond in the heart of Londesborough Park attracts a variety of wildfowl

at a three-fingered Yorkshire Wolds Way signpost where you rejoin the main route and walk straight ahead up to **Londesborough**.

Follow the road through the village, passing All Saints Church.

> There are no facilities for walkers in the village of **Londesborough**. There are lovely cottages and houses to admire in the village, and All Saints Church is a feature of interest. The present Londesborough Hall is a brick-built structure. In 1819 the Duke of Devonshire ordered the demolition of the original stone-built Londesborough Hall so that materials could be taken across country and incorporated into Chatsworth House in Derbyshire.

Turn right to take a road up from the village, straight through a crossroads, then across a gently sloping landscape of cultivated fields. Although the land barely reaches 90m (295ft) there is a view indicator to help unravel the distant features seen across the Vale of York. In clear weather this view stretches from Goole Docks to York Minster and Pocklington Church, taking in prominent

power stations at Doncaster, Drax, Eggborough and
Ferrybridge. The heights of the Peak District and Yorkshire
Dales mark the furthest horizon.

Turn right a short
way uphill at a
road junction,
then turn
left along
the farm
access
road to
**Partridge
Hall**. Turn

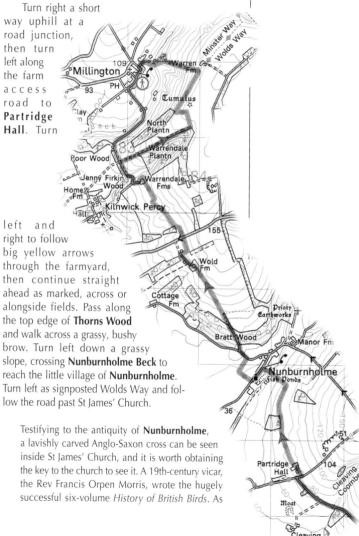

left and
right to follow
big yellow arrows
through the farmyard,
then continue straight
ahead as marked, across or
alongside fields. Pass along
the top edge of **Thorns Wood**
and walk across a grassy, bushy
brow. Turn left down a grassy
slope, crossing **Nunburnholme Beck** to
reach the little village of **Nunburnholme**.
Turn left as signposted Wolds Way and follow the road past St James' Church.

Testifying to the antiquity of **Nunburnholme**,
a lavishly carved Anglo-Saxon cross can be seen
inside St James' Church, and it is worth obtaining
the key to the church to see it. A 19th-century vicar,
the Rev Francis Orpen Morris, wrote the hugely
successful six-volume *History of British Birds*. As

its name suggests, Nunburnholme was indeed the site of a nunnery – the Benedictine Priory of St Mary. A 12th-century manorial complex has been identified, and there are Tudor earthworks and the remains of a fishpond. There are no facilities for walkers, apart from a Tuesday-only bus linking Nunburnholme with Pocklington and Huggate.

Turn right to follow a path alongside a field. The path itself later turns right and reaches another minor road. Turn left to follow the road then right at a junction. A rather battered road climbs steeply uphill through **Bratt Wood**. Go through a gate and walk along the full length of a cows' field to leave at another gate on the far side. Continue through fields and follow the marked route through a farmyard at **Wold Farm**. Leave along the farm access road but turn right uphill beside a house. Turn left along the edge of a field to reach the B1246. ◄ Simply cross the road to continue, as signposted for the Wolds Way.

Drop downhill from the road a short way and walk straight ahead alongside fields, but make a quick turn

Buses run to and from Pocklington, 3km (2 miles) off-route, but could be difficult to stop. There is a B&B halfway down the road.

Last view of the Wolds Way before moving off-route to the village of Millington right and left at a small gate signposted Wolds Way. Note another distinctive 5-mile marker post. Follow a track and pass behind the buildings at **Warrendale Farm**, where camping is available, before turning left down the farm access road. The road reaches a junction where a decision needs to be made if lodging is required. A left turn by road leads off-route to **Kilnwick Percy** and Pocklington, while walking straight ahead along the road short-cuts to **Millington**.

Kilnwick Percy lies slightly off-route, although some parkland and a substantial old hall might just be glimpsed. Kilnwick Percy Hall was first mentioned in the Domesday Book of 1086, although the present building is late-18th century. The estate fell on hard times and part of the hall was demolished, but the remainder has been restored as the Madhyamaka Buddhist Centre. Visits to the hall might be limited to one tour per month, but the grounds and gardens can be explored daily. There is a café on site and accommodation is available.

The busy little market town of **Pocklington** lies 3km (2 miles) off-route, but has a good range of services if walkers need more than the basic facilities offered in the little Wolds villages. It has a couple of hotels offering food, drink and accommodation, and there are banks with ATMs, a post office, plenty of pubs and restaurants, and lots of shops. East Yorkshire buses regularly link Pocklington with York, Market Weighton, South Cave, Beverley and Hull, as well as a service crossing the Wolds Way on the road to Driffield. A Tuesday-only bus links Pocklington with Nunburnholme and Huggate.

To continue along the Wolds Way, turn right up a track and climb beside **Warrendale Plantation**. The gradient eases at the top, then turn left to walk straight across a field. Turn left at a big marker post, walk downhill a short way, then turn right to continue alongside a field with a view down to Millington, as well as further afield to Sutton Bank in the North York Moors and to the distant Pennines. Leave the Wolds Way at a kissing gate on the left, walking straight down a steep slope. Don't follow a track on the right, but follow a path and go down a few steps. Follow a plastic duckboard across wet ground in a small wood. Walk up a track, which soon swings left to join a road at Dalehead Cottage on the way into **Millington**.

MILLINGTON

This is a small and attractive village. The Ramblers Rest is a café with accommodation. Laburnum Cottage and Garthend House also offer accommodation. The Village Hall provides basic lodgings, with camp-beds, toilets and a kitchen. Breakfast can be provided on request. The Gait Inn offers evening meals.

STAGE 4
Millington to Thixendale

Start	Ramblers Rest, Millington (SE 831 518)
Finish	Cross Keys, Thixendale (SE 845 610)
Distance	19.5km (12 miles)
Time	6hr
Terrain	Several ascents and descents across dales, with some short, steep stretches early in the day. Easy roads, tracks and paths through cultivated fields most of the rest of the day.
Maps	OS Landrangers 100 and 106, OS Explorers 294 and 300
Refreshments	Pub at Huggate. Café at Fridaythorpe. Pub at Thixendale.
Public transport	A Tuesday-only bus links Pocklington with Huggate. East Yorkshire buses offer infrequent midweek links between Fridaythorpe and Driffield.

This day's walk leads well into the heart of the Yorkshire Wolds, first on a roller-coaster route up and down the steep slopes of the dales, then enjoying views across huge field systems, with the 'big sky' feeling of spaciousness. Huggate is the first village passed during the day's walk, and although it lies just off-route, most walkers are happy to detour to visit the Wolds Inn. The village is in a remote setting, is quaint and charming, and provides basic services. Fridaythorpe is the next village and the route goes straight through it. While it is interesting, it is also on a busy main road, so it isn't as quiet. At the end of the day Thixendale is a remarkable retreat, hidden among a veritable maze of grassy dales, and an ideal place to spend the night. However, facilities are sparse and it's best to book beds in advance.

Leave **Millington** via the Ramblers Rest and Laburnum Cottage to reach Dalehead Cottage. Turn right at a road junction, then right again down a track. Just before reaching a house at the bottom, follow a path and use a plastic duckboard to cross wet ground in a little wood. Go up few steps, then climb straight uphill, avoiding a track to the left. Re-join the Yorkshire Wolds Way at a kissing gate on top, turning left to follow it.

A tall hedgerow obscures views on the way towards **Warren Farm**, where the farm access road is crossed. The Wolds Way continues alongside another field, following an old earthwork at around 190m (625ft). Swing left to descend alongside the field, then go through a gate and drop more steeply into the grassy Sylvan Dale. The route crosses the dale and climbs steeply in a sweeping zigzag, signposted to the right and left. ◄

In recent years this was a direct ascent, but it became too steep, worn and slippery.

Enjoy a brief respite at the top of the slope while walking alongside another field and following the line of another **earthwork**. There is another steep descent, this time using a path running along the opposite side of a fence to a clear track. Cross grassy Nettle Dale and follow the path alongside the fence up the other side. Turn right to walk up a grassy path on a slope covered in bushes, continuing alongside

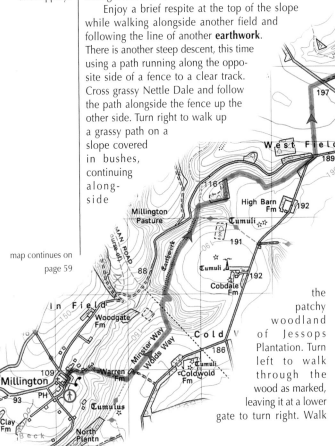

map continues on page 59

the patchy woodland of Jessops Plantation. Turn left to walk through the wood as marked, leaving it at a lower gate to turn right. Walk

alongside a fence along the top of a steep-sided grassy valley known as the Huggate Sheepwalk. The fence leads to another patch of woodland and a gate takes the route onto a minor road. Turn left to walk to a nearby road junction.

Simply cross over the road junction to follow a grassy path gently uphill through **West Field**. The route passes a 5-mile marker post, rises to over 205m (675ft) and joins a clear track. Turn right to follow the track to a road and cross over to follow the access road towards **Glebe Farm**. Don't walk close to the buildings, but turn right as marked beforehand, continuing down the access road to reach a road junction. The Wolds Way turns left here, but most walkers will be happy to turn right and go up through the lovely and peaceful village of **Huggate**.

The delightful little village of **Huggate** lies deep in the heart of the Wolds and is a fine place to take a break. The whitewashed Wolds Inn, at 165m (540ft), offers food, drink and accommodation as well as camping. A small post office with limited opening times sells sweets and ice cream. A Tuesday-only bus links Huggate with Nunburnholme and Pocklington.

Walk down the road away from Huggate, then gently uphill and along a tree-lined avenue with neatly mown edges that leads towards **Northfield House**. Turn left before reaching the house, as signposted alongside a field, at around 165m (540ft). Go through a small gate in a hedge and drift right to follow a path down the flank of an attractive grassy dale. The path slices across an ancient **earthwork** on its way to the floor of **Horse Dale**. Go through a gate in a fence at the bottom and turn left to walk up along the grassy floor of Holm Dale.

Towards the top of the dale, branch right up a smaller dale and go through a gate at the top to reach a track in a patch of woodland. Turn right to follow the track, which becomes a narrow road leading to the main A166 into the village of **Fridaythorpe**. Turn right to follow the main road into the village, then turn left to reach a quiet green and duck pond.

Fridaythorpe sits astride a busy road but has some quaint corners worth discovering. The box-like church, while being of no great antiquity, was built on a Norman foundation. A notice on the green near the duck pond marks the halfway point of the Wolds Way, as well as celebrating the 21st anniversary of the route and recording its re-launch

Walkers climb through grassy Holm Dale on their way to Fridaythorpe

in 2004 as the Yorkshire
Wolds Way. The trail was
first declared open on this
green, while more recently
a walkers' shelter was
installed.

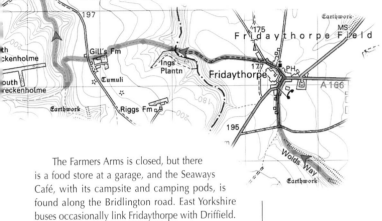

The Farmers Arms is closed, but there
is a food store at a garage, and the Seaways
Café, with its campsite and camping pods, is
found along the Bridlington road. East Yorkshire
buses occasionally link Fridaythorpe with Driffield.

Follow a minor road away from the green, out of
Fridaythorpe, passing the ABN Feed Mill. A track runs
alongside the mill and the Wolds Way continues alongside a field. Go through a gate and follow a clear path
slicing down across a steep and grassy slope into a dale,
and continue past **Ings Plantation**. Go through another
gate, where there is a 5-mile marker post, and turn left to
walk up through a smaller dale. Reach a track at a higher
level and follow it, turning left only for a short way, then
right and straight ahead again to walk alongside the trees
surrounding **Gill's Farm**. Cross a minor road at around
210m (690ft).

The Wolds Way runs straight onwards then turns left
to follow a clear track that slices straight down across a
steep grassy slope into a long dale. ▶ Turn sharp right at
the bottom of the slope to walk down through the dale,

Note a spiral
earthwork on the
floor of the dale.

Thixendale Village Hall serves refreshments on Sundays

which bends left and right, passing a tree house. The grassy floor of the dale and a clear track lead to a road where the Wolds Way is signposted to the right. The road runs through a dale cut deep into **Thixendale Wold** and walkers should keep left at road junctions to enter the straggly village of **Thixendale**, near the Cross Keys.

THIXENDALE

It has been suggested the village's name means 'six dales' or even 'sixteen dales'. One thing is certain – a confusing maze of steep-sided grassy dales branches outwards from the village. Since land suitable for extensive ploughing and planting is limited, the area is largely given over to sheep rearing rather than cultivation.

Facilities in Thixendale include the Cross Keys pub, offering food, drink and accommodation. The Village Hall serves refreshments on Sundays and there is a small shop opposite.

STAGE 5
Thixendale to Sherburn

Start	Cross Keys, Thixendale (SE 842 611)
Finish	Sherburn (SE 958 767)
Distance	30.5km (19 miles)
Time	9hr
Terrain	Easy roads, tracks and paths throughout the day, but several ascents and descents, with some short, steep slopes.
Maps	OS Landrangers 100 and 101, OS Explorer 300
Refreshments	None on the route, but just off-route, North Grimston has a pub and the Wolds Way Lavender Farm has a café. Another pub lies off-route at West Heslerton. There is a pub, restaurant and takeaway at Sherburn.
Public transport	The Moors Explorer is a summer Sunday-only bus passing through Wharram le Street, linking Hull and Beverley with Malton and Danby. Yorkshire Coastliner buses link West Heslerton, East Heslerton and Sherburn with Ganton, Filey and Scarborough, as well as Malton, York and Leeds.

The route remains very much in the heart of the Yorkshire Wolds, wandering through the dales, in and out of woodlands and traversing huge field systems. A highlight of the day is the deserted village of Wharram Percy, where it is worth spending time exploring. Only two other villages are passed, Wharram le Street and Wintringham, although neither provide any facilities. It is possible to move off-route to North Grimston, which has a pub, or visit Wolds Way Lavender Farm near Wintringham, which has a café. Towards the end of the day, if Sherburn seems too far away, walkers can drop down off-route to West Heslerton or East Heslerton in search of food, drink, lodging, or buses further off-route.

Walk all the way through the village of **Thixendale** almost as far as Manor Farm, but turn right beforehand up a chalky track, slicing up across the steep slopes of **Beamer Hill**. Don't approach the farm buildings tucked away in a small woodland, but turn left as signposted at a track junction and go through a gate. Continue along the track across **Cow Wold** at around 200m (655ft). Turn left as signposted, following a path just inside a field, instead of following the track any further. The path later turns right and drops into a grassy dale.

Walk across the dale as marked and head straight up through a smaller dale and go through a gate at the top. Walk alongside a field and into a patch of woodland to reach a prominent junction of tracks at around 215m (705ft). Turn right as

map continues on page 64

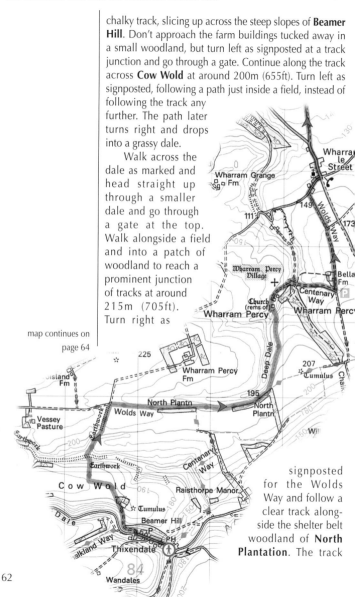

signposted for the Wolds Way and follow a clear track alongside the shelter belt woodland of **North Plantation**. The track

A restored millpond and picnic site at the deserted village of Wharram Percy

WHARRAM PERCY

Take time to study the noticeboards around the site of this famous medieval deserted village. Most people head straight for the ruins of St Martin's Church, which is the most obvious remnant of the village, and thereby miss the outlines of several ancient dwellings on the higher grassy slopes. There are traces of prehistoric and Roman occupation, while the original timber church was a 10th-century Saxon construction.

The outline of the North Manor, South Manor and peasant farmsteads can be traced by referring to the noticeboards around the site. The only house still standing is relatively modern, but it was built on the site of an 18th-century farmstead. It is used by archaeologists working on the site. As for the church, it was in use until 1949, but was inconveniently located away from surrounding villages. The tower fell down in 1959 and the ruins have since been consolidated.

map continues on
page 67

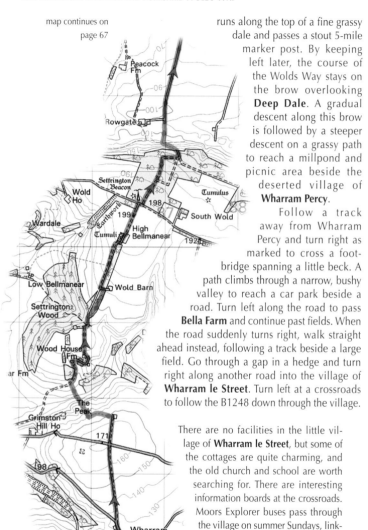

runs along the top of a fine grassy dale and passes a stout 5-mile marker post. By keeping left later, the course of the Wolds Way stays on the brow overlooking **Deep Dale**. A gradual descent along this brow is followed by a steeper descent on a grassy path to reach a millpond and picnic area beside the deserted village of **Wharram Percy**.

Follow a track away from Wharram Percy and turn right as marked to cross a footbridge spanning a little beck. A path climbs through a narrow, bushy valley to reach a car park beside a road. Turn left along the road to pass **Bella Farm** and continue past fields. When the road suddenly turns right, walk straight ahead instead, following a track beside a large field. Go through a gap in a hedge and turn right along another road into the village of **Wharram le Street**. Turn left at a crossroads to follow the B1248 down through the village.

There are no facilities in the little village of **Wharram le Street**, but some of the cottages are quite charming, and the old church and school are worth searching for. There are interesting information boards at the crossroads. Moors Explorer buses pass through the village on summer Sundays, linking Hull and Malton, then reaching Danby in the North York Moors.

Continue along the B1248 to leave Wharram le Street, then turn right up a clear track through fields to reach the B1253. ▶ This is known locally as High Street and runs to 171m (561ft); cross it and continue along another track towards buildings. Keep left into a field and turn left to follow the field boundary. Go through a kissing gate and follow a fence along the top of another field at **The Peak**, then drop to the right as signposted and cross a footbridge over a tiny stream. There is another 5-mile marker post here. Walk up to a farm access road and turn right.

Walk up through a stable-yard at **Wood House Farm**, climbing higher to reach a triangular track junction. Turn right alongside a woodland, as signposted for the Wolds Way. Leave the track at a kissing gate to follow a path along the edge of the wood, rising gradually parallel to a track. Later, turn left to follow the track through the shelter belt woodland, then turn right to follow it gently uphill. Another quick right and left turn leads through the yard of **High Bellmanear Farm**. The dirt access road leads onwards at a height of 199m (653ft) to reach a road junction at **Settrington Beacon**, where there is a covered reservoir.

Turn right along the road, then almost immediately left into a forest to follow a clear track gently downhill. This eventually turns right among pines and beeches, then watch for a path signposted down to the left, leading to a gate out of the forest. At the top of a grassy slope a bench offers a fine view of the route ahead and far across the plains beyond.

Follow an obvious grassy groove of a track down a steep slope and swing right through a hollow filled with nettles, although these don't impinge on the track. Cross a rise and follow a dirt road straight ahead, away from the nearby farm of **Rowgate**, dropping gently into a broad vale. Turn right as marked at the bottom, walking alongside a field and straight across another field. Cross a footbridge over Wintringham Beck and pass an attractive little pond on the way to a road in the village of **Wintringham**.

Either road could be used to reach the village of North Grimston, 2.5km (1½ miles) off-route, which has a pub/B&B and a campsite.

The parish church in Wintringham is a prominent landmark on the Wolds Way

There are several pretty cottages in **Wintringham** and the parish church is full of interest and well worth a visit, but there are no facilities for walkers. However, the Mill House offers accommodation, and the Wolds Way Lavender Farm has a café offering food and drink, both 1km (½ mile) off-route. Ryedale Community Transport operates a Tuesday-only bus linking Wintringham with Malton.

Turn left along the road to leave Wintringham, then turn sharp right along a track known locally as Back Side, skirting the village alongside fields, almost reaching the church and road at the other end of the village, as well as a 5-mile marker post. Turn left here, away from the

church, following a field path up to a track. Turn left
along the track and follow it across the foot of a wooded
slope. Quickly swing right and climb through **Deep Dale
Plantation**, which has a mixture of beech and pines.
When the track suddenly bends left, turn right instead
and climb steeply. Notice how the signposts at the top
and bottom are angled, reinforcing the steepness of the
slope!

Go through a rustic gate to leave the forest and have
a look at a huddle of strange wooden figures – an artwork
called 'Enclosure Rites'. The path runs along the top of
an ancient **earthwork** flanked by bushes. Cross an access
road, turning quickly left and right as signposted for the
Wolds Way. ▶

There is an option
to turn right to reach
the nearby Wolds
Way campsite
at West Farm.

Walk straight towards **Knapton Wood** and follow a
clear path to the right, just inside the wood. Later leave
the wood to cross a grassy gap where a small valley cuts
the wooded brow. The route continues alongside another
wood on West Hesterton Brow, and later turns right to
run parallel to a minor road before suddenly turning left
to cross it. This road could be followed steeply downhill
and off-route to **West Heslerton**, where there is a pub.

Views across the Vale
of Pickering extend
to the North York
Moors and the coast.

Staying on the Wolds Way, follow a gravel track
alongside a small pine forest and turn
left around its boundary, then
turn right to walk along the
grassy **East Heslerton
Brow** to around 180m
(590ft). ▶ Watch for
quick left and right
turns later, and

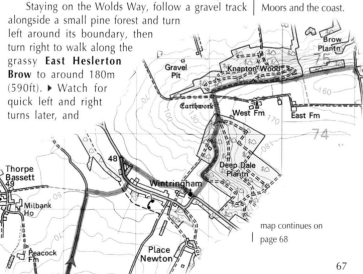

map continues on
page 68

A wooden sculpture – 'Enclosure Rites' – stands near West Farm

continue walking alongside a fence, passing a viewpoint bench. Keep to the left of a woodland that surrounds **Manor Wold Farm** and hides it from view, then cross the farm access road. This road offers a descent off-route to **East Heslerton** in search of lodgings.

West and East Heslerton lie downhill and off-route, so most Wolds Way walkers don't visit them. A small range of facilities is available, with West Heslerton offering pub accommodation and East Heslerton offering farmhouse accommodation. Both villages are served by regular Yorkshire Coastliner buses, allowing rapid links with other villages and towns offering more services, from Malton to Filey and Scarborough.

Continue along East Heslerton Brow, crossing a field away from Manor Wold Farm. Follow a grassy track alongside a hedge and a wood, then turn left a short way downhill and right to walk alongside a coniferous plantation. Notice two graves in a corner at the far end of the plantation, then watch for the Wolds Way turning left downhill a short way. Turn right as signposted, and while the path is vague it basically follows a line of trees across the wooded slope – no doubt the remains of an ancient hedgerow. Turn right at a stout 5-mile marker, climbing steeply from **Crowsdale Wood**, levelling out at another patch of woodland beside a road at around 150m (490ft).

Turn left to follow the road gently downhill to a junction at the top of **Sherburn Brow**. The Wolds Way runs parallel to the road, across a wooded

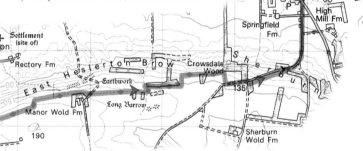

slope, then re-joins the road to continue downhill. The road is called Whitegates and it levels out as it leads off-route to the nearby village of **Sherburn**. Walkers who wish to stay on the Wolds Way should turn right along a clear track that simply runs from one road to another, although most will be happy to visit the village and avail of its services.

SHERBURN

Sherburn appeals because it provides a small range of services in an area largely bereft of food and drink. St Hilda's Church is also interesting, with its Norman tower and examples of Saxon statuary.

Facilities include a post office store, pub, takeaway, shop and campsite. Yorkshire Coastliner buses run from Leeds and York to Filey and Scarborough, linking Sherburn with the nearby villages of West and East Heslerton and Ganton. Although a railway runs past Sherburn, there is no station.

STAGE 6
Sherburn to Filey

Start	Sherburn (SE 958 767)
Finish	Coble Landing, Filey (TA 120 809), or Filey Brigg (TA 126 816)
Distance	24 or 26km (15 or 16 miles)
Time	7hr 30min or 8hr
Terrain	Mostly gentle field paths, farm tracks and quiet roads, although there are some short, steep descents and ascents while crossing dales.
Maps	OS Landranger 101, OS Explorers 300 and 301
Refreshments	Café at Potter Brompton. Ganton and Muston each have a pub. Plenty of pubs, restaurants, cafés and takeaways around Filey.
Public transport	Yorkshire Coastliner buses link Sherburn, Ganton and Filey with York and Leeds. East Yorkshire buses link Filey with Muston, as well as running all the way back to Hull. Trains run from Filey to Scarborough and York, as well as back to Hessle and Hull.

The Wolds Way leaves Sherburn and stays fairly low through Potter Brompton and Ganton, then climbs high over the top of Staxton Wold. Several small grassy dales are crossed or followed, before the route finally descends from the high ground. The little village of Muston is followed by the busy seaside resort of Filey – a place that has little in common with the Wolds. Essentially the walk along the Yorkshire Wolds Way is over, and all that remains is a short stroll out onto the crumbling clay promontory of Filey Brigg. Those who only intend to walk the Wolds Way will double back to Filey. However, those who wish to keep walking will probably stay overnight in Filey, then walk to Filey Brigg the following morning and continue along the coast to Scarborough.

Walkers leaving **Sherburn** find themselves at a fork in the road. To the right is Whitegates – the road that was followed into the village the previous day. To follow every part of the Wolds Way, walkers should go back up this road and turn left along a clear track. However, if they take the other fork they will quickly re-join the Wolds Way where the track reaches the road not far from **High Mill**. Either way, continue along the road up to another fork and turn left. Another left turn reveals a path running across a slope of grassy areas and patchy woodlands. Follow the route as signposted across the slope, sometimes without any views, if the woods on either side are particularly dense. Turn right uphill later, then left at a small gate to walk down a woodland path.

Emerging from the wood, walk down through fields and turn right, soon passing between a coniferous shelter belt and a small golf course. Turn right to follow a track through the fields to reach attractive buildings in the little farming hamlet of **Potter Brompton**. ▶ Turn right along a road, then almost immediately left along a clear track running alongside more fields at the foot of the slope. Eventually, turn left down a minor road, away from Ganton Hall and its extensive grounds. Turn right at a junction to walk alongside the village of **Ganton**, keeping right of St Nicholas' Church and its 14th-century spire.

Turn left towards the main A64 road, if a break at a farm café/bakery appeals.

An attractive old stone building in the farming hamlet of Potter Brompton

The **Ganton** Greyhound Inn is located on the main A64 road, offering food, drink and accommodation. There is a campsite at Windlebeck Farm. The names of some of the houses speak of more facilities in the past, such as 'The Old Shop' and 'The Old Post Office'. Yorkshire Coastliner buses link Ganton with Filey, Sherburn, Malton, York and Leeds.

Follow a field path straight away from St Nicholas' Church, crossing a track and later going through a gap in a shelter belt woodland. Turn right uphill until a left turn is signposted alongside a field. This leads to a clear track called Wold Lane, which is followed straight uphill to the right. Pass a stout 5-mile marker post and the track narrows as it approaches **Binnington Wold Farm**. Turn left well before the farm as signposted at the corner of a field, then later turn right at a small gate to walk beside another field. Turn left again at another small gate and walk beside another field to reach the busy B1249 road at **Staxton Wold Farm**. Continue straight onwards as signposted along a private road. This leads to the military installation of **RAF Staxton Wold**, where walkers turn right and pass alongside the security fence at 178m (504ft).

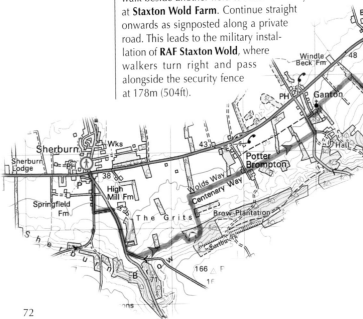

RAF STAXTON WOLD

This military installation seems incongruous in the peaceful Wolds. It claims to be the oldest radar station in the world, constructed in 1939, just in time to monitor airborne activity during the Second World War. However, it was almost destroyed by the RAF themselves in 1942 when a Halifax bomber had to drop all its explosives near the site while executing an emergency landing because of a fire onboard. It is one of a number of early warning stations located throughout eastern England. Apparently, it stands on the site of a third-century early warning beacon site constructed by the Romans!

The road becomes a track as it leaves the site, passing High Farm and dropping into a small wooded dale. Watch for a turning on the left towards the bottom, then climb a steep path on a wooded slope. The gradient soon eases and a fence leads onwards beside a field. Turn right around a corner of the field, then turn left to walk beside another field. Drop into a small grassy dale, climb up the other side, then cross a smaller dale. Cross the slopes of **Flixton Wold**

map continues on page 74

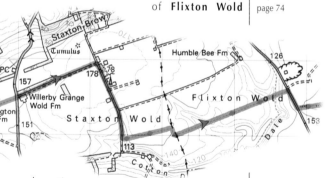

and continue straight across larger **Lang Dale**. All these dales are likely to be used for sheep grazing, while all around are cultivated fields. Follow the line of a fence along the remains of an old hawthorn hedge to reach a minor road. ▶ Turn right to follow the road over a rise just above 150m (490ft).

The luxury campsite of Humble Bee Farm, with its cottages, cabins, yurts and wigwams, is located nearby.

Turn left to leave the road as signposted for the Wolds Way and walk along the brow of Raven Dale. A path follows the line of a fence and an ancient **earthwork**. There is a short, steep descent into **Camp Dale**, closely following the fence. Note the scrub woodland on the left that fills the head of the dale. Turn right and rise gradually across the side of the dale. A couple of marker posts are followed by a more obvious 5-mile marker post and a bench. Pass along the foot of a wooded slope while gradually swinging left reaching some rumpled earthworks known as **The Camp**, at a confluence of dales.

Keep left as signposted to walk up through Stocking Dale, where patchy scrub woodland covers the valley sides. Keep to the grassy floor of the dale until the route leaves it, then turn right as signposted to walk

Bright poppies grow profusely among the crops on the way to Stockendale Farm (Yorkshire Wolds Way, Stage 6)

alongside a belt of woodland planted on top of a linear earthwork. Turn left along an uncomfortably stony track to pass **Stockendale Farm** and reach a minor road at almost 130m (425ft).

There is barely a glimpse ahead to Filey, although the more distant Scarborough and Flamborough Head are clearly in view.

Cross over the road and walk along a track beside a shelter belt woodland close to **Muston Wold Farm**. Bear right as signposted later, across a field then through a gate and down beside more fields, through a couple more gates. This is the final descent as the Yorkshire Wolds gradually peter out. ▸ The path appears to be heading for the A1039 road, but turns right and runs parallel to it, passing West Farm. When the road is joined, walk along West Street into **Muston**, to pass the Ship Inn, then continue along King Street to pass All Saints Church.

Facilities are limited in the pretty little village of **Muston**, where the Yorkshire Wolds Way is rapidly coming to a close. The Ship Inn offers food and drink. East Yorkshire buses regularly link Muston with Filey, Scarborough, Bridlington and Hull.

On the way out of Muston watch for a Wolds Way signpost on the left, beside a few steps, indicating a short field path that leads from the A1039 to the busier A165. Cross over the road and continue along another field path, continuing close to a school sports field. Cross a footbridge and turn right along a track between the sports field and some houses, reaching the A1039 again. Turn left to follow this road – called Muston Road – into **Filey**.

The course of the Wolds Way through Filey isn't always clear, so keep an eye open for street names. Muston Road leads from the suburbs to a level crossing near the station, where Station Avenue continues into town, reaching a roundabout beside a bus station. Continue along the avenue, then turn left along Union Street, then right along Mitford Street. Turn left along Reynolds Street and right along Queen Street to reach the town council offices. At the end of the street, a path and steps drop to a coastal road and promenade. Across the road is the **Coble Landing**, where fishing boats are brought up from the beach. ◄

'Coble' is pronounced 'cobble'.

If your plan is simply to complete the Yorkshire Wolds Way, then all that remains is to walk another 1km (½ mile) to Filey Brigg (see 'Route to Filey Brigg', below). If planning to continue walking, and complete one or both of the other trails in this guidebook, then it is more likely that a night will be spent in Filey, leaving a visit to Filey Brigg until the following day.

FILEY

Filey is a little fishing town that has turned its attention to tourism. On the Coble Landing, fishing boats lie on trailers beside amusement arcades, as if the transition is not yet complete. The town is fairly small but supports a good variety of services, whether walkers are at the end of the Yorkshire Wolds Way or about to begin the Cleveland Way.

Facilities include a range of accommodation and a nearby campsite. There are banks with ATMs, a post office, toilets, plenty of pubs, restaurants, cafés and takeaways, as well as shops. The museum should be visited by anyone wanting a potted history of the town. There is a tourist information centre on John Street, tel 01723 383636, www.discoveryorkshirecoast.com/filey.

East Yorkshire buses regularly link Filey with Scarborough as well as Muston, Bridlington and distant Hull. Yorkshire Coastliner buses regularly link Filey with Malton, York and Leeds, passing the Wolds Way villages of Ganton, Sherburn, East and West Heslerton. Trains run from Filey to Scarborough as well as back to Hessle and Hull.

Route to Filey Brigg

Just inland from the Coble Landing is Church Ravine, with a road running up it. Leave the road and walk up a zig-zag path featuring well over 100 steps on a wooded slope, then continue along a low, grassy cliff-top path. This passes above Filey Sailing Club, then over 100 steps drop into the little **Wool Dale** and over 100 more steps climb from it.

Continue along the grassy cliff path through **Filey Country Park** and walk out onto the crest of **Filey Brigg** to enjoy the sea breeze. A nearby stone sculpture is carved with the names of highlights from two National Trails. At this point, those finishing the Yorkshire Wolds Way will head back into Filey, but those who wish to continue along the Cleveland Way and Tabular Hills Walk can continue towards Scarborough and the North York Moors National Park.

FILEY BRIGG

The grassy top of Filey Brigg has been crumbling steadily over the centuries and will one day be gone, leaving only the hard calcareous gritstone bedrock beneath. A Roman signal station and 12th-century castle have already been lost as the clay cliffs have crumbled, and walkers are now asked not to continue along the badly worn and dangerous clay ridge down to the rocky slabs of Brigg End. To visit the end of the Brigg, you should do it by walking along Filey Sands when the tide is out. Bear in mind that the rocks are covered in slippery seaweed and big waves sometimes break across them without warning. There is an emergency telephone for those who find themselves marooned out on the point or spot anyone in obvious difficulty or danger.

STAGE 7

Filey to Scalby Mills
(via the Cleveland Way)

Start	Coble Landing, Filey (TA 120 809)
Finish	Old Scalby Mills (TA 036 908)
Distance	18.5km (11½ miles)
Time	5hr 30min
Terrain	Straightforward cliff coast walking leads to a rugged wooded slope, then urban walking along streets, roads and promenade paths.
Maps	OS Landranger 101, OS Explorer 301, Harvey Cleveland Way
Refreshments	Beach hut and surf shop at Cayton Bay. Plenty of pubs, restaurants, cafés and takeaways around Scarborough.
Public transport	East Yorkshire buses run all around Scarborough, while buses 120 and 121 operate between Filey and Scarborough. Northern trains run between Filey and Scarborough.

This day's walk is essentially a link route, using a stretch of the Cleveland Way to link the end of the Yorkshire Wolds Way with the beginning of the Tabular Hills Walk. This is a fine one-day walk in its own right, with stretches of cliff coast between the resorts of Filey and Scarborough. The route is fairly straightforward, but isn't actually waymarked or signposted through Scarborough. Most walkers would be happy to follow the promenade round Castle Cliff, but it is worth climbing over the headland, using paths and flights of steps to include a visit to Scarborough Castle. Scalby Mills lies just to the north of Scarborough, where walkers can start the Tabular Hills Walk.

Leave **Filey** as if heading inland by road from the **Coble Landing**, into Church Ravine. Walk up a zigzag path featuring well over 100 steps on a wooded slope, then continue along a low, grassy cliff-top path. This passes above Filey Sailing Club, then over 100 steps drop into the

little **Wool Dale** and over 100 more steps climb from it. Continue along the grassy cliff path through **Filey Country Park** and walk out onto the crest of **Filey Brigg** to enjoy the sea breeze. (See end of previous section for information about Filey Brigg.) A nearby stone sculpture is carved with the names of highlights from two National Trails, where the Yorkshire Wolds Way meets the Cleveland Way.

Follow an easy, grassy cliff path past the Rocket Pole, along **North Cliff**, eventually turning around **Cunstone Nab**. Steps cross

The promontory of Filey Brigg can be explored when the tide is out

map continues on page 81

an earth bank, then walk past a mobile home site while heading gently downhill along **Gristhorpe Cliff**, then turn around the headland of Red Cliff

79

The sandy sweep of Cayton Bay is barely glimpsed from the wooded slopes

Between the houses and cottage there is access inland to a surf shop that sells sweets and ice cream.

Point, enjoying fine views ahead to Scarborough. The path climbs over the top of **Lebberston Cliff**, reaching 80m (260ft) above sea level, then descends and runs seawards of a row of houses and a cliff-top cottage. ◀

Walk down to cross a beach access road above **Cayton Bay**, noting that there's a beach shop just off-route. Climb again, then turn right and walk down a steep, stone-pitched path on **Tenants Cliff**. Turn left to continue along the coast path and note the Second World War pillboxes, some of which have toppled from the crumbling clay cliffs on which they were built. The Cleveland Way wanders across a wooded slope with occasional flights of steps. Keep an eye on route markers, as some paths lead off-route down to the beach. ◀

Geologists might like to detour to Cornelian Bay in the hope of picking semi-precious stones from the beach.

Turn left up flights of wooden steps, counting well over 100 before reaching a road at **Osgodby**. This is virtually a suburb of Scarborough, but the Cleveland Way avoids the built-up sprawl as much as possible. Turn right and follow the A165 road, then turn right again at some houses to regain the cliff edge at **Knipe Point**. Turn left and continue along a grassy path beside the edge of a woodland at the top of **Frank Cliff**. The path later crosses a duckboard and joins a track.

Turn right down a track as if heading for the beach, but bear left to climb 45 stone steps and turn around the small headland of **White Nab**. Keep to the 'rough' around the edge of a golf course, close to a crumbling clay cliff that displays numerous landslips. The path later runs across a wooded slope and emerges just below a car park at the end of Sea Cliff Road. The Holbeck Hall Hotel once stood nearby.

The **Holbeck Hall Hotel** was built as a private residence in 1880 and later converted into a hotel. Unfortunately the ground beneath the building was unstable and began to slump on 3 June 1993 – an event that was documented as it happened by TV crews. The following day the hotel was in ruins and about a million tonnes of material had slumped into the sea in a huge bulge. An information board beside the Sea Cliff Road car park shows

map continues on page 82

before and after pictures of the event, and the area has since been landscaped.

Black Rocks

White Nab

Cornelian Bay

Frank Cliff

Osgodby Point

Cayton Cliff

Osgodby PH

Tenants' Cliff

Cayton Bay

Calf Allen Rocks

Cow Leys Fm

Lebberston Cliff

Yons Nab

Castle Rocks

Mount Pleasant Fm

High Dale Cott

Redcliffe Fm

Tumulus

Cliff Fm

Walk down a path, where landslip material bulges towards the sea, and has been landscaped. Take careful note of the tide and the state of the sea, because the route stays low all the way to Scarborough, but notices warn that high seas can break over the sea walls. If it looks dangerous to proceed, there are plenty of paths and roads at a higher level that can be used instead, and walking through the Holbeck Gardens and South Cliff Gardens is an attractive option.

If following the sea wall, the route soon passes the 'Star Disk'. It doesn't look much, but anyone visiting at night-time will see a number of stars and constellations illuminated over a wide area of the ground, representing the night sky. There is no waymarked or signposted route for the Cleveland Way through Scarborough, but the sea wall leads around **South Bay** and soon passes **The Spa** complex, where it joins a road.

Ahead lies the big, brash, bustling resort of **Scarborough**, and without an 'official' route in and out of the town, a number of options present themselves. The simplest option smacks a little of 'cheating', which is to catch one of the open-top

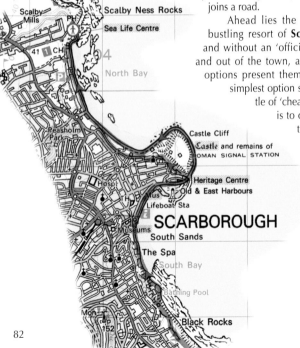

Suncruiser buses from South Bay to North Bay. The simplest alternative on foot is to walk along the promenade, first following Foreshore Road around **South Bay** to reach the **Old Harbour**, then following Marine Drive around the headland at the foot of **Castle Cliff**, before Royal Albert Drive completes the journey around **North Bay**.

Detour to explore Scarborough

Those who wish to see more of Scarborough's history and heritage should explore uphill and inland. For instance, there's a fine geology **museum** at the Rotunda, which can be seen from the promenade through the arches of the Spa Bridge, near the imposing Grand Hotel. Once a roundabout at the far side of the harbour is reached, paths and flights of steps can be used to reach **Scarborough Castle**.

> Bronze Age settlers are thought to have been the first to fortify the headland at Scarborough. The Romans operated a signal station on a line of sight linked with other coastal signal stations at Ravenscar and Filey Brigg. In the 12th century **Scarborough Castle** was built on the headland. The castle withstood a 20-day siege during the Pilgrimage of Grace in 1536, but surrendered after a year-long siege during the Civil War in 1645. The ruins of the castle can be visited while exploring the town. There is an entrance charge, tel 01723 372451.

Not far from the castle is St Mary's Church, where visitors search the churchyard for Anne Brontë's grave. Unless a visit to the town centre appeals, roads such as Blenheim Terrace and Queens Parade link with paths leading down to the end of Royal Albert Drive on North Bay. The road heads inland, offering access to the delightful **Peasholm Park**.

To continue along the coast, simply follow a promenade path onwards beside **North Bay**. Buildings quickly give way to rows of beach huts. Later, the promenade path bends markedly as it passes the Sea Life Sanctuary, www.visitsealife.com/scarborough. Traffic, including local bus services, turns around here, and just beyond the turning area is the Old Scalby Mills pub. **Scalby Mills** itself lies just inland, offering a small amount of accommodation, including a youth hostel and campsite.

SCARBOROUGH

The emergence of Scarborough as a holiday resort can be traced to the promotion of its spa waters. In 1626 a local doctor extolled the benefits of drinking the water, making so many claims about its curative properties that one must suspect quackery! However, visitors flocked to the town and before long the benefits of sea air and sea bathing were also being promoted. So enthusiastic were the crowds of holidaymakers that more and more facilities had to be built to cater for them. The arrival of the railway in 1845 boosted the tourism trade and the town remains a busy and bustling place to this day.

Facilities around Scarborough include a wide range of accommodation options, from splendid hotels to humble bed-and-breakfasts, as well as a youth hostel at Scalby Mills and nearby campsites. There are banks with ATMs, post offices, toilets, and an abundance of pubs, restaurants, cafés and takeaways to suit all tastes, although in many cases it's 'chips with everything'. As a shopping centre Scarborough has the greatest choice of any place visited in this guidebook. The tourist information centre is on Burniston Road, near Peasholm Park, tel 01723 818111, **www.discoveryorkshirecoast.com/scarborough**. Trains run to a number of destinations throughout the country, including to Filey, Hull, York and Leeds. Yorkshire Coastliner buses link Scarborough with York and Leeds. Arriva buses link Scarborough with Robin Hood's Bay, Whitby, Guisborough and Middlesbrough. East Yorkshire buses link Scarborough with Scalby Mills and the Sea Life Sanctuary, for the start of the Tabular Hills Walk. East Yorkshire buses link Scarborough and Filey, as well as heading inland to Helmsley for the start of the Cleveland Way.

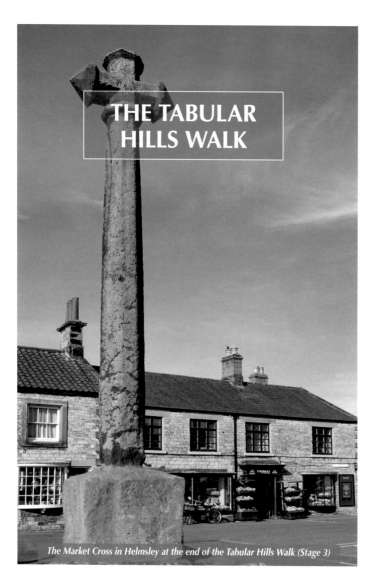

THE TABULAR HILLS WALK

The Market Cross in Helmsley at the end of the Tabular Hills Walk (Stage 3)

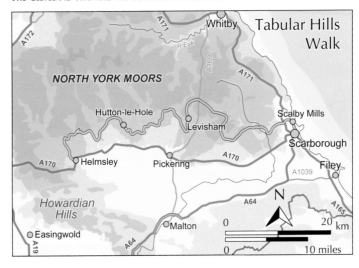

The Tabular Hills stretch along the southern part of the North York Moors National Park. The land rises gently from south to north and is cut by a series of dales that leave tabular, or 'table-like', uplands between them. The gentle slope often ends abruptly at its northern end in a series of shapely knolls, or 'nabs', that look northwards to the rolling moorlands at the heart of the National Park.

The rocks making up the Tabular Hills belong to the Middle Oolite group in the Corallian series of the Jurassic period and are around 170 million years old. They are essentially a limestone and lime-rich sandstone series, porous enough to allow surface water to drain away rapidly, and are seldom exposed. In the more deeply cut dales the bedrock is the older Oxford Clay, which is impervious and supports the flow of rivers and streams. While some parts of the Tabular Hills have been turned over to commercial forestry, the land is very fertile and easily ploughed. The soil is often too thin to support good root crops, but grain crops such as wheat, barley and oats are grown in rotation, rustling in the wind, and oilseed rape crops blaze yellow early in summer.

The idea for creating a link between Scalby Mills and Helmsley, to convert the enormous loop of the Cleveland Way into a circular walk, originated in 1974. The route was worked out by Malcolm Boyes, then he and several others walked along it in 1975, calling it the 'Missing Link'.

The Tabular Hills Walk seeks to achieve the same thing, and although

A view from Levisham Moor and Saltergate into the heart of the North York Moors (Stage 1)

the course of this route differs in places, the main villages visited by both routes are the same. Walkers can either start with the Tabular Hills Walk and continue along the Cleveland Way, or walk the Cleveland Way first and complete a full circuit by following the Tabular Hills Walk afterwards. Signposts and waymarks for the Tabular Hills Walk feature a directional arrow and a 'Tabular Hills' logo. The route has been designated as a regional trail and is an initiative of the North York Moors National Park Authority.

The Tabular Hills Walk logo

STAGE 1
Scalby Mills to Levisham

Start	Old Scalby Mills (TA 036 908)
Finish	Horseshoe Inn, Levisham (SE 833 906)
Distance	33.5km (21 miles)
Time	10hr
Terrain	Generally easy paths, tracks and minor roads through fields and forest, ending with a moorland walk.
Maps	OS Landrangers 94, 100 and 101, OS Explorer OL27
Refreshments	Pub at the start. Pubs in Scalby. Café at Everley. Café off-route in Danby Forest. Pub at Levisham.
Public transport	East Yorkshire buses regularly link Scarborough with Scalby Mills and the Sea Life Centre. Arriva buses also serve Scalby from Scarborough and Whitby. Yorkshire Coastliner buses regularly pass the Hole of Horcum between Whitby and Malton.

Technically, the Tabular Hills Walk begins where a footpath heads straight inland from the coastal Cleveland Way to the village of Scalby Mills. Although the Scarborough Youth Hostel makes a good starting point, by setting off from Old Scalby Mills, walkers can follow a short stretch of the coastal path before heading inland, with no need to double back on themselves. Bear in mind that facilities are limited throughout this day and the full distance to Levisham may not be within the capability of all walkers. If intermediate accommodation is needed there is a solitary B&B at South Moor Farm, beside Dalby Forest, over halfway through the day.

Start at the pub at Old Scalby Mills, near the Sea Life Sanctuary, and cross a footbridge over a river. Two flights, totalling 75 stone steps, reveal the coastal path running northwards around **Scalby Ness**. Don't be tempted inland too early along a path overlooking a valley, but continue a little further along the coast path. The start of the Tabular Hills Walk is signposted straight inland for Helmsley.

Follow a path alongside two fields to reach the busy A165 Burniston Road and turn right. ▶ Turn left along Field Lane, passing the entrance to the Scarborough Camping and Caravanning Club Site. Pass a roundabout and Field Lane becomes Station Road as it enters **Scalby**. When the busy A171 Scalby Road is reached, either turn left to follow it downhill or walk straight along High Street to explore the centre of the village first.

Turn left down the road to reach the Scarborough Youth Hostel at Scalby Mills.

Facilities at **Scalby** include a couple of pubs, a shop, a café and toilets. Accommodation is limited to the nearby youth hostel and campsite, but Scalby is close to Scarborough, which has abundant accommodation. East Yorkshire buses regularly serve the village from Scarborough, while Arriva buses regularly serve the village from Scarborough and Whitby. The railway through the village operated only from 1885 to 1965, and now serves as a footpath and cycleway to Whitby.

Walk down the busy main road only to cross a bridge over a river, then turn right to walk alongside, following a grassy path. The river has obviously been artificially cut through the landscape and is flanked by earth embankments. The **Sea Cut**, as it is known, looks rather like a canal with a towpath.

map continues on page 91

THE SEA CUT

The River Derwent has its source on Fylingdales Moor, a mere spit and a throw from the North Sea. It flows towards the sea, but only 6km (3¾ miles) short of it, suddenly swings west and heads far inland. Its waters eventually spill into the North Sea via the River Humber after a circuitous journey of 240km (150 miles). The Sea Cut was engineered by the distinguished inventor Sir George Cayley (a pioneer in the science of aerodynamics, amongst other things) in the early 18th century. It diverts the headwaters of the River Derwent into Scalby Beck, passing floodwater straight to the sea, preventing it from inundating the Vale of Pickering. The Sea Cut also provided a good head of water for industry at Scalby Mills.

Cross a road at a bridge on the outskirts of the village and walk along another stretch of grassy path. This leads through a strip of woodland beside the Sea Cut, then there are open fields beyond and good views back towards the prominent little hill of Scalby Nab. Cross a bridge beside the attractive **Mowthorpe Farm**, then follow a minor road gently uphill to pass the **Everley** Country House Café.

Follow the road gently downhill and turn left along another minor road signposted for **Wrench Green**. The road crosses the River Derwent, swinging right and left, passing the Old Chapel as it climbs through the hamlet. A steeper climb leads into woodlands,

map continues on page 93

then the tarmac road levels out and proceeds as a gravel road into **Wykeham Forest**. Turn right at a junction of tracks, then left at a fork to keep to the clearest gravel road, which is also waymarked as the Moor to Sea cycleway. A viewpoint car park is reached at Highwood Brow, at a junction with another narrow tarmac road at an altitude of 208m (682ft).

Walk straight along the road, passing a turning for the Raptor Viewpoint. ▸ The fields beside the road near **Brompton Moor House** produce millions of tree seedlings every year. Just before reaching the entrance to the Wykeham Forest **Nurseries**, branch right along a clear track marked for the Tabular Hills Walk. Pass more tree plots and follow the track as it gradually descends to a car park and a narrow tarmac road near **Cockmoor Hall**. Take a moment to study rumpled ground nearby – the **earthworks** are the remains of the ancient Cockmoor Dikes.

Birdwatchers could make a brief detour here, adding 1km (½ mile) to the day's walk.

> Over a dozen embankments and ditches run parallel at the **Cockmoor Dikes**, and a study of a detailed map reveals other ancient linear earthworks in the same area. These include the Scamridge Dikes and Oxmoor Dikes, thought to have been constructed by rival tribes to mark their territories.

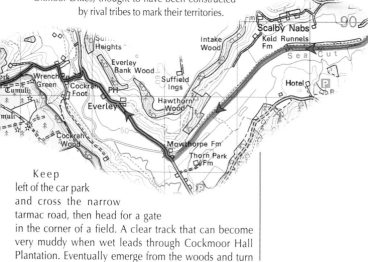

K e e p left of the car park and cross the narrow tarmac road, then head for a gate in the corner of a field. A clear track that can become very muddy when wet leads through Cockmoor Hall Plantation. Eventually emerge from the woods and turn

A long and straight track is followed on the way towards Givendale Head Farm

right along a road, passing the **Oxmoor Dikes** earthworks while enjoying views across open fields. The road leads straight towards **Givendale Head Farm**.

Continue along a broad gravel forest road, later taking a right fork past a field used as a campsite. ◄ Pass the access road for Ebberston Common Farm and the gravel road later leads straight onto a minor road. Follow this ahead, noting that **South Moor Farm**, on the right, offers bed and breakfast in this remote location. Follow the road only until it bends to the right, and instead keep straight ahead along a gravel forest road signposted for Crosscliff.

Turning left off-route leads to a coffee shop, if their signboard is displayed.

Walk along and gently down the forest road, which gradually bends left through **Crosscliff Wood**, then turn right as signposted for disabled parking to reach a junction of tracks. Avoid all the tracks at this junction and walk straight along a path signposted as an 'easy access trail', to pass a viewpoint at 233m (764ft). The prominent hump of Blakey Topping can be seen across the dale, and it is one of the more shapely heights on the otherwise gently rolling expanses of the North York Moors.

Continue along the path and keep straight ahead along a forest track on Crosscliff Brow. The track is attractively lined with deciduous trees that screen most of the nearby commercial conifers from view. There are occasional glimpses of Blakey Topping, then better views of the hill once the track goes through a gate and continues along the grassy Newgate Brow. ▶ Pass another gate to join and follow uphill a farm access road. This is known as Old Wife's Way and leads to the busy A169

Lying well off-route to the south are the celebrated Bride Stones, weathered into bizarre forms.

road near Saltergate.

Cross the main road with care and turn right to follow a path overlooking the **Hole of Horcum**. The path runs parallel to the main road but at a safe distance from the traffic. Poor, marshy fields seen below are flanked by bushy hedgerows and patchy woodlands, with heather moorland all around the head of the valley.

map continues on page 94

93

THE HOLE OF HORCUM AND THE SALTERSGATE INN

According to a locally favoured legend, a giant by the name of Wade was out of sorts with his wife, and scooped up a pile of earth to throw at her. He missed, and the resulting hole became the Hole of Horcum, while the lump of earth became Blakey Topping. The former Saltersgate Inn used to be visible from a gap at the head of the Hole of Horcum. Regular Yorkshire Coastliner buses pass Saltergate if walkers need to leave the route, linking Whitby with Lockton and Pickering.

Saltergate was an important trading route running inland from the coast. It was also known as the Salt Road or Fish Road. Smugglers took illicit goods along it and were in the habit of holing up at the Saltersgate Inn. According to local lore revenue men raided the place one night, but the smugglers ensured that nothing was discovered. However, one revenue man who lingered too long afterwards was killed and his body was buried beneath the hearthstone of the inn. The landlord of the day insisted that a fire be kept continually ablaze to deter anyone from digging up the hearthstone, and this tradition was maintained for generations afterwards. The ever-blazing fire at 'The Legendary Saltersgate Inn' became a tourist attraction in its own right! Sadly, the fire was finally quenched in 2007 when the pub closed. The building was finally demolished in 2018.

map continues on page 95

Go through a gate and follow a moorland track a short way uphill from the Hole of Horcum, soon levelling out around 270m (885ft) on **Levisham Moor**. There is only one clear track across the undulating heather moorland, so route-finding errors are

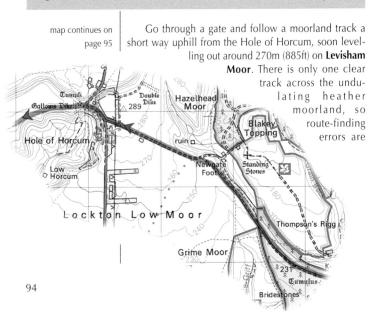

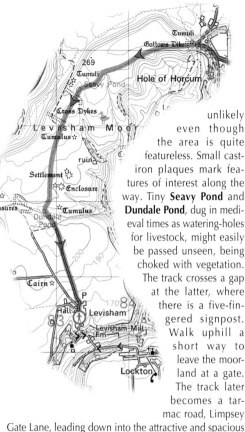

unlikely even though the area is quite featureless. Small cast-iron plaques mark features of interest along the way. Tiny **Seavy Pond** and **Dundale Pond**, dug in medieval times as watering-holes for livestock, might easily be passed unseen, being choked with vegetation. The track crosses a gap at the latter, where there is a five-fingered signpost. Walk uphill a short way to leave the moorland at a gate. The track later becomes a tarmac road, Limpsey Gate Lane, leading down into the attractive and spacious village of **Levisham**.

LEVISHAM AND LOCKTON

The village has a broad central green surrounded by stout stone cottages and farmhouses.

Facilities include the Horseshoe Inn for food, drink and accommodation, as well as Rectory Farm B&B. There is a youth hostel at nearby **Lockton**, across a valley, along with a tearoom. Regular Yorkshire Coastliner buses serve Lockton from Whitby, Saltergate, Pickering, Malton and Leeds.

STAGE 2

Levisham to Hutton-le-Hole

Start	Horseshoe Inn, Levisham (SE 833 906)
Finish	Ryedale Folk Museum, Hutton-le-Hole (SE 705 900)
Distance	24.5km (15¼ miles)
Time	7hr 30min
Terrain	Muddy paths at first, then mostly clear tracks and roads. Some short ascents and descents across wooded dales with large fields in between.
Maps	OS Landrangers 94 or 100, OS Explorers OL26 and OL27
Refreshments	Pubs at Newton-on-Rawcliffe, Cropton, Appleton-le-Moors and Hutton-le-Hole.
Public transport	Bus services are sparse and school services are only available to permit holders. Monday-only Stephensons buses link Newton-on-Rawcliffe, Cropton, Appleton-le-Moors and Hutton-le-Hole with Pickering. Wednesday-only Ryedale Community Transport buses link Appleton-le-Moors and Hutton-le-Hole with Kirkbymoorside and Marton. Summer Sunday Moors Explorer buses link Hutton-le-Hole with Danby, Pickering and Hull. Summer weekend Moorsbus services link Hutton-le-Hole with Pickering, Danby and Guisborough. Regular East Yorkshire buses link Helmsley and Pickering with Scarborough.

After the rather remote first day's walk, this stage of the Tabular Hills Walk includes a succession of charming little villages, and each one features at least a pub offering food and drink, as well as a couple of accommodation options. The route crosses the North York Moors Railway, where steam-hauled trains may be spotted. The railway and surrounding area featured regularly in the popular television series *Heartbeat*. At the end of this stage the Ryedale Folk Museum at Hutton-le-Hole is well worth exploring. Over a dozen cottages, houses, farms and shops feature life throughout the ages in this part of Yorkshire, with plenty of supporting artefacts and implements on display.

Walk down through **Levisham** to the bottom end of the village. Follow a path straight downhill, cutting out a sweeping bend to land on the road at a lower level. Turn left along the road, then turn right along a track as signposted. The ruin of St Mary's Church lies down to the left, and it can be visited by making a short detour. If not, keep straight ahead along a muddy track inside a wood.

> **St Mary's Church** stands on an 11th-century foundation and is tucked deep in a steep-sided valley. It seems rather remote from Levisham village. According to legend it was supposed to be built in the village, but each night the Devil carried all the building materials down into the valley. The church was virtually abandoned before the tower was added, and a new church was built in 1884 at a more convenient location in the village.

The route varies from a muddy woodland track to a grassy path, passing through a succession of gates and eventually reaching a three-way signpost in a field. Turn left and pass through two gates to cross two footbridges – first

The ruins of St Mary's Church lie deep in a valley below the village of Levisham

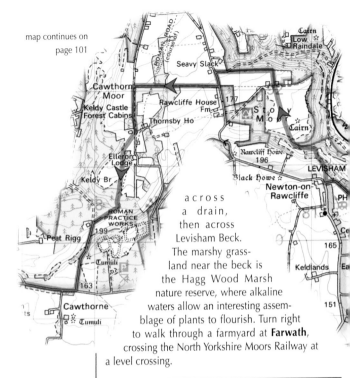

map continues on
page 101

a c r o s s
a drain,
then across
Levisham Beck.
The marshy grass-
land near the beck is
the Hagg Wood Marsh
nature reserve, where alkaline
waters allow an interesting assem-
blage of plants to flourish. Turn right
to walk through a farmyard at **Farwath**,
crossing the North Yorkshire Moors Railway at
a level crossing.

NORTH YORKSHIRE MOORS RAILWAY

This scenic railway runs between Pickering and Grosmont, a distance of
29km (18 miles), and is famous for its steam-hauled services, although
when it opened in 1836 the carriages were actually horse-drawn. The line
was engineered by George Stephenson but had to be improved considerably before steam trains could use it. Although closed in 1964, it was sub-
sequently re-opened by a group of dedicated railway enthusiasts and is now
an immensely popular tourist attraction. Scenes involving the line feature
regularly in period films and on television, including the long-running
'Heartbeat' series. Trains do not stop at Farwath, but Levisham Station can
be reached by walking down into wooded Newton Dale from the village of
Newton-on-Rawcliffe. For details of services on the line, tel 01751 472508,
www.nymr.co.uk.

Cross another footbridge, or a culvert bridge, over **Pickering Beck** and follow the clear farm access track of Farwath Road up across a wooded slope. It emerges at a junction of farm access roads where a right turn leads past Howlgate Farm and **Howlgate Nab**. Keep to the farm access road to pass **East Brow House** and reach the top end of **Newton-on-Rawcliffe**, close to a road at 190m (625ft).

Newton-on-Rawcliffe features a splendid, spacious green with a duck pond, surrounded by stone farmhouses and cottages. Facilities include a pub called The White Swan, offering meals and a campsite. Swan Cottage, Pond Farm and Elm House Farm provide bed and breakfast accommodation. Monday-only Ryedale Community Transport buses link Newton-on-Rawcliffe with Cropton and Pickering.

Turn right at the top end of the village without even touching the road if local facilities are not required. A track crosses a rise, then it may be muddy for a short while before dropping down the steep, wooded Newton Banks into a valley. Go through a gate and ford a beck, then follow a boulder-studded path up **Stony Moor**, where there is patchy woodland as well as heather and bilberry. ▶

Cross a track and go through a gate to the left of a cottage near Middle Farm. Continue along a grassy path through woodland. Turn left at an intersection of paths and walk straight ahead, out of the wood and through fields. Continue along a clear track to a road near **Seavy**

This area represents what the North York Moors looked like before large swathes were converted to farmland or heather moorland.

Slack and turn left. Walk only a short way down the road and turn right along a clear track known as the Peat Road, heading for **Cawthorn Moor**, touching 200m (655ft).

When a T-junction is reached, turn left to walk down a woodland track and cross an access road. Go through a small gate and walk diagonally across a field, passing a solitary tree to reach a corner of a wood. Follow a clear path down through the wood and cross a footbridge over **Sutherland Beck**. Turn right to follow a path uphill, then walk along the inside edge of the wood to reach a road and farm at Keldy. Turn left to follow the road up a wooded slope where the rumpled earthworks of a **Roman Practice Works** lie out of sight to the left, on a wooded hill.

> The Romans advanced rapidly through Britain during the first century AD, subduing the country by superior military might. They established a **military practice camp** on Cawthorn Moor. The lack of any defensive works suggests that the local inhabitants were in no mood to attack the site.

Turn right after crossing the highest part of the road to follow High Lane, which has broad grassy verges. The road reaches its highest point at 178m (584ft), then descends and swings left down into the village of

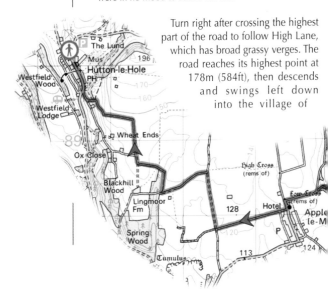

Cropton. The Tabular Hills Walk actually heads down to the right just as High Farm, which offers bed and breakfast, is reached. Walk down a delightfully overgrown old lane, passing St Gregory's Church.

> A motte and bailey was built at **Cropton** in the 12th century, but it was in ruins by the end of the 14th century. St Gregory's Church may have been built on a Norman chapel site, but while it retains its 12th-century font, the building is essentially a 19th-century restoration.
>
> Facilities in the village include the New Inn, offering accommodation, camping, meals and tours of its thriving micro-brewery. High Farm also offers accommodation. Monday-only Ryedale Community Transport buses link Cropton with Newton-on-Rawcliffe and Pickering.

Turn right down a steep road, away from the village, then turn left along a clear track as signposted. When the track suddenly turns right, leave it by walking straight ahead to enjoy a fine, garlic-scented woodland path, passing through a number of gateways. Eventually, at a junction of paths turn right down to the **River Seven** and cross it using

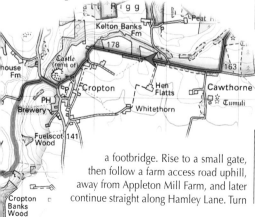

a footbridge. Rise to a small gate, then follow a farm access road uphill, away from Appleton Mill Farm, and later continue straight along Hamley Lane. Turn left at a road junction beside the stump of an old stone cross to approach **Appleton-le-Moors**. The route actually turns right just as it reaches the substantial Dweldapilton Hall on the outskirts of the village.

Appleton is a typical Yorkshire 'croft and toft' village. The crofts are the little cottages arranged on either side of the long main street, the tofts are the pieces of land extending out at the back of each dwelling where householders would grow their own vegetables. The imposing Dweldapilton Hall was built by a wealthy whaler, and 'Dweldapilton' was an earlier name for the village.

Facilities include the Moors Inn, offering food, drink and accommodation. Monday-only Ryedale Community Transport buses link Appleton-le-Moors with Hutton-le-Hole, Pickering and Kirkbymoorside. Wednesday and Saturday buses link Appleton-le-Moors with Hutton-le-Hole, Malton and Kirkbymoorside.

Houses are arranged around extensive greens at Hutton-le-Hole

Follow the track away from the hall, eventually reaching a prominent junction of tracks. Turn right through a gate and follow an unenclosed track gently uphill through fields. Turn left along Lingmoor Lane as signposted, at another prominent junction of tracks. Walk through a gate and approach a wood. There are two gates ahead, so be sure to go through the one on the right, into the wood. Turn right to walk around the inside edge of the wood, then continue through fields. Turn right along another clear gravel track, Bottomfields Lane, rising gently. Turn left at the top and continue along a grassy track through more fields. The track then drops steep and narrow, goes through a gate and down to a road. Turn right to walk up into the charming village of **Hutton-le-Hole**.

HUTTON-LE-HOLE

Hutton-le-Hole has a long history of settlement dating back to Neolithic times. The village was mentioned in the Domesday Book as Hoton, and throughout the ages has also been rendered as Hege-Hoton, Hoton under Heg, and Hewton. As a place name Hutton-le-Hole dates only from the 19th century.

Facilities in this lovely village, which has splendid greens with a stream running through, include the interesting Ryedale Folk Museum. Accommodation is available at The Crown, Burnley House and The Barn. The Crown and a couple of tea shops offer food and drink. Monday-only Stephensons buses link Hutton-le-Hole with Appleton-le-Moors, Cropton, Newton-on-Rawcliffe and Pickering. Wednesday-only Ryedale Community Transport buses link Hutton-le-Hole and Appleton-le-Moors with Kirkbymoorside and Marton. Summer Sunday Moors Explorer buses link Hutton-le-Hole with Danby, Pickering and Hull. Summer weekend Moorsbus services link Hutton-le-Hole with Pickering, Danby and Guisborough.

RYEDALE FOLK MUSEUM

You can trace the history of Yorkshire folk from 4000BC to 1953, with plenty of hands-on exhibits, as you wander from one part of the Ryedale Folk Museum site to another. Over a dozen buildings have been erected since 1964, some supported by enormous cruck frames (pairs of curved wooden timbers supporting the ends of the roof), many standing in isolation, while

Reconstructed shops and dwellings are a feature of the Ryedale Folk Museum

others are arranged as a row of small shops. Vintage vehicles, including motorised and horse-drawn carriages, are preserved, and land around the site sprouts vegetables and flowers, including many varieties of cornfield flowers. Local people often give demonstrations of traditional crafts while wearing period dress. There is an entrance charge, and the museum incorporates a shop, toilets and tourist information centre, tel 01751 417367, www.ryedalefolkmuseum.co.uk.

STAGE 3

Hutton-le-Hole to Helmsley

Start	Ryedale Folk Museum, Hutton-le-Hole (SE 705 900)
Finish	Market Cross, Helmsley (SE 613 839)
Distance	22km (13½ miles)
Time	6hr 30min
Terrain	Mostly clear paths, tracks and roads crossing a succession of dales, fields and woodlands.
Maps	OS Landrangers 94 or 100, OS Explorer OL26
Refreshments	Pub at Gillamoor. Plenty of choice around Helmsley.
Public transport	Monday-only Ryedale Community Transport buses link Pickering with Hutton-le-Hole, Gillamoor, Fadmoor and Kirkbymoorside. East Yorkshire buses link Helmsley with Pickering and Scarborough. Reliance buses link Helmsley with Kirkbymoorside and York daily, except Sunday.

The route crosses a succession of dales on its way from Hutton-le-Hole to Helmsley. A few of these are small and might barely be noticed, but others are larger and deeper, flanked by steep wooded slopes. A couple of charming little villages are passed, but for the most part the route is without facilities until the end of the day at Helmsley. The widest range of services occurs at that point, as well as immediate access to the Cleveland Way for those hardy walkers who feel that their exploration of the North York Moors has only just commenced.

Follow the road uphill through **Hutton-le-Hole**, reaching a road junction near the last buildings. Turn left as signposted through a gate, then immediately turn right. A well-marked path passes through small fields to reach a little area of moorland. Follow only the waymarked path downhill, avoiding all others, and cross a footbridge on the way towards **Grouse Hall**.

Keep well to the left of the farm, walking through fields and down to the **River Dove**. Cross a footbridge

Gillamoor is one of a series of charming farming villages passed by the Tabular Hills Walk

and pass an old mill restored as a dwelling. The access road leads up to a wooded slope where it bends right. Turn left up a path as signposted, emerging from the woods beside St Aidan's Church in **Gillamoor**, which has a fine viewpoint alongside. Walk straight through the village, passing the Royal Oak Inn, and continue along the road to reach the neighbouring village of **Fadmoor**.

The charming little villages of **Gillamoor** and **Fadmoor** lacked a reliable water supply until the 18th century, when Joseph Foord engineered a lengthy aqueduct that tapped into distant sources of water and channelled a supply to the

map continues on page 108

villages. This supply was still in use in the 20th century until it was replaced by piped water.

Facilities in Gillamoor include the Royal Oak Inn for food, drink and accommodation, as well as Manor Farm for bed and breakfast. Fadmoor has a spacious green, but no services for walkers, following the closure of its pub. Both villages are served by Monday-only Ryedale Community Transport buses, linking with Hutton-le-Hole, Kirkbymoorside and Pickering.

Turn left as signposted for Kirkbymoorside, then turn right along a road signposted for Sleightholmedale. At the next road junction, turn right again as signposted for Sleightholme Dale. The road is called Green Lane and it runs through an avenue of trees. Follow the road gently downhill then turn left along a track beside **Mell Bank Wood**. Pass a signpost and follow the track away from the

Old buildings lying deep in wooded Kirk Dale alongside Hold Cauldron Mill

map continues on
page 109

woods, through fields. Later, turn right as signposted and the track drops down a wooded slope. Keep left in the woods to reach a stone bridge and a former corn mill at **Hold Cauldron**, deep in **Kirk Dale**.

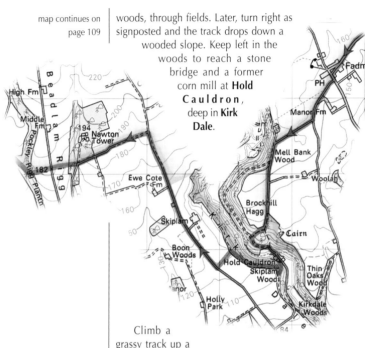

Climb a grassy track up a steep, wooded slope, following a power line away from the old mill. At the top of the slope turn sharp right to walk along a delightful grassy track between the wooded slope and higher fields. The track rises very gently, but as soon as it starts to descend, watch for a small gate on the left bearing a waymark. Walk straight across fields to reach a minor road and turn right to follow it gently uphill through fields.

Pass the farm access roads for **Skiplam Grange** and **Ewe Cote Farm**. Turn left as marked at a road junction, where there is a tiny memorial and a small plantation of trees. The road runs straight through fields, with the house of **Nawton Tower** briefly seen on the right. ◄

When a road junction is reached walk straight down a woodland path signposted as a bridleway. Cross

Surrounding woodland has been cleared of rhododendron, with some trees fells and other trees planted.

the little valley of **Howl Dale** and climb up the other side to walk through fields. Cross a road on **Beadlam Rigg** and follow a track through fields. Drop into the wooded Pinderdale to pass through the narrow **Pockley Rigg Plantation**.

Cross a track and follow the path up out of the valley and into the higher fields to cross another minor road. Follow a track that bends left towards a wood then swings right and drops down the wooded slope into **Riccal Dale**. Turn left towards a farmhouse at **Hasty Bank**, leaving the track just beforehand, keeping right of the building. Keep left of a crumbling building and cross a footbridge over the **River Riccal**.

Walk only a short way downstream before going through

a gate, then turn right uphill using a narrow but clear path on a forested slope. Pass a

109

A track runs through Ash Dale towards Helmsley.

bench, cross a track and climb steeper and higher. Turn left as signposted along a muddy track that soon runs along the edge of the forest. It reaches a junction with a concrete road, quickly followed by a tarmac road near **Carlton Grange**.

Turn left to follow the tarmac road over a rise and walk almost to the farming hamlet of **Carlton**. There are no facilities here for walkers and the route is signposted to the right just before the buildings are reached. A clear gravel track called Keld Lane runs straight past fields before swinging right to drop into **Ash Dale**. Turn left to follow a track along the grassy floor of the valley, with steep wooded slopes on either side.

There is no way of gauging progress down the winding dale, but much later watch for a narrow, signposted path on the right. Go through a gate to leave the woods and walk alongside a field. Go through another gate and turn right, then go through yet another gate and turn left. Turn right in a corner of a field and walk until a gate on the left gives access to a narrow tarmac path. Walk into **Helmsley** and a Tabular Hills Walk signpost will be seen pointing back to Scalby. Either turn left along a road to reach the youth hostel, or right to reach All Saints Church, then keep left to enter the Market Place and finish at the Market Cross. This is the end of the Tabular Hills Walk, but it is also the start of the Cleveland Way.

HELMSLEY

Fine old shops and buildings are clustered around Helmsley's Market Place

Helmsley is a quintessential Yorkshire market town tracing its ancestry back to Anglo-Saxon times. The spacious Market Place fills with stalls on market day and serves as a car park at other times. Apart from the Market Cross there is a towering monument to the second Lord Feversham. Stout stone buildings stand on all sides of the Market Place, and a couple of poky alleys lined with quaint little shops lead away. The most prominent building is the Town Hall. All Saints Church is just outside the Market Place, founded in Norman times but essentially a 19th-century structure.

Helmsley is the largest town on the Tabular Hills Walk and offers the fullest range of facilities. There is a good range of accommodation, banks with ATMs, post office, toilets, plenty of pubs, restaurants and tearooms, as well as shops galore, including an outdoor gear store. Bus services include regular East Yorkshire buses linking with Pickering and Scarborough, and Reliance buses linking with Kirkbymoorside and York daily, except Sunday. Summer weekend Moorsbus services run to Sutton Bank, Rievaulx and Guisborough.

The ruins of Helmsley Castle are passed by the Cleveland Way

HELMSLEY CASTLE

Not every visitor to Helmsley is aware of Helmsley Castle, despite its proximity to the town centre. It was built around 1200 and saw plenty of strife in 1644 during the Civil War. Colonel Crosland held the castle for the Crown, while Sir Thomas Fairfax led the besieging Parliamentarian force. Fairfax was hit by a musket ball during one assault and his siege was threatened by a Royalist force from Knaresborough Castle. This relief force was beaten back and harried as far as Black Hambleton, which might be construed as an early attempt to cover the Cleveland Way! The castle surrendered towards the end of 1644 and was rendered useless during 1646 and 1647 when parts of the keep and walls were destroyed. It is managed by English Heritage and there is an entrance charge, tel 0870 3331181.

THE CLEVELAND
WAY NATIONAL
TRAIL

Black Nab is an isolated sea stack beyond Saltwick Bay (Stage 7)

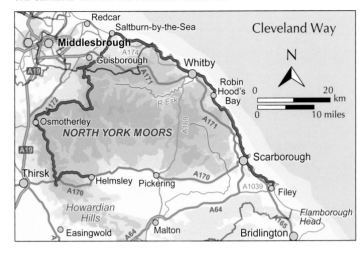

The Cleveland Hills form the western slopes of the North York Moors National Park. The hills rise to no great height, with only a few summits exceeding 400m (1300ft), but all rise abruptly from the plains. Views from these hills are therefore a stark contrast between agricultural lowlands and wild, open heather moorlands in the heart of the North York Moors. The moorlands have long been man-managed in the interest of grouse shooting and represent the largest extent of heather moorland in the country. Views from the eastern cliff coastline also offer a contrast, this time between the intricate agricultural landscape, cleft by wooded valleys and the North Sea, with its seaside resorts where fishing is giving way to tourism.

The rocks making up the Cleveland Hills and coast are generally from the lower and middle Jurassic periods, and are some 170–200 million years old. The lower beds include Lias shales and ironstones, which have been extensively quarried, whereas the higher moorlands are generally capped by sandstones from the Ravenscar group, although there are crumbling shale beds too. The sandstones effectively protect the lower rocks and determine the plateau-like structure of the North York Moors. To the southwest, around Helmsley and Osmotherley, the slightly younger rocks of the oolite group are exposed – more dramatically so than in the Tabular Hills. Much of the bedrock in the northeast and southeast of the area is buried beneath deep deposits of ill-sorted glacial drift and alluvium.

The Cleveland Way was the second national trail to be established in Britain (the Pennine Way was first) and it was officially opened in 1969. The route was devised as a loop around the North York Moors National Park, starting from Helmsley and taking in the steep scarp slope overlooking the plains in the west, all the way to Guisborough, before hugging the cliff coast from Saltburn to Filey to the east. The contrast between the open moorlands and the cliff coast, with its succession of bustling seaside resorts, means that the trail is essentially two completely different experiences. Even at the outset some walkers questioned whether this trail should have been a circular walk, finishing back at Helmsley, but since that time the Tabular Hills Walk has been waymarked and is there to be walked if anyone chooses to complete a full circuit. The option also exists, of course, to finish the Cleveland Way at Filey Brigg and immediately embark upon the Yorkshire Wolds Way.

Waymarks for the route are the standard National Trail 'acorn' logo, along with directional arrows. Signposts for the route may simply read 'Cleveland Way', or they may additionally give one of the next destinations along the trail. Keep up-to-date with developments and diversions by checking the Cleveland Way website, www.nationaltrail.co.uk/cleveland-way, and download a current copy of the *Cleveland Way Accommodation and Information Guide*.

A path leads to Roseberry Topping (Stage 5)

STAGE 1
Helmsley to Sutton Bank

Start	Market Cross, Helmsley (SE 613 839)
Finish	National Park Centre, Sutton Bank (SE 515 830)
Distance	17km (10½ miles)
Time	5hr
Terrain	Easy walking along clearly marked paths and tracks, from wooded dales to open fields and cliff edges.
Maps	OS Landranger 100, OS Explorer OL26, Harvey Cleveland Way
Refreshments	Café at Sutton Bank National Park Visitor Centre.
Public transport	East Yorkshire buses link Helmsley with Pickering and Scarborough. Reliance buses link Helmsley with Kirkbymoorside and York daily, except Sunday. Moorsbus offers summer weekend links between Helmsley, Sutton Bank and Guisborough.

The first day along the Cleveland Way sees the route leaving Helmsley and crossing over a wooded rise to Rievaulx, where a short detour takes in the substantial ruins of Rievaulx Abbey. The route climbs from wooded valleys to higher fields, reaching a steep western scarp slope at Sutton Bank. Another short detour along the cliff edge of Roulston Scar takes in Kilburn White Horse, then the route doubles back on itself to allow an exploration of the National Park Visitor Centre at Sutton Bank. Lodgings are scarce around Sutton Bank, but walkers who make an early start from Helmsley could press on towards High Paradise Farm or even distant Osmotherley for the night, making a day of 36km (22½ miles).

Leave the Market Cross at Market Place in **Helmsley** by following the road signposted for Stokesley, passing All Saints Church. Turn left along a road called Cleveland Way, signposted 'Footpath to Rievaulx'. Note the Cleveland Way signpost and a stone sculpture beside the Cleveland Way car park, deeply carved with the names of some

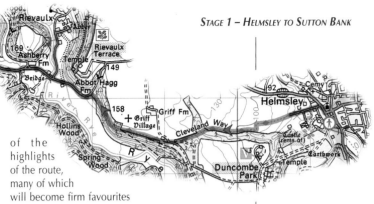

of the highlights of the route, many of which will become firm favourites in the days ahead as wayfarers follow the trail.

Follow a clear track, keep right at a junction and head gently uphill. Continue along the clearest footpath through fields, using kissing gates. The route is well way-marked, turning left and right at signposts to run parallel to a wood. Later, the path drops into the wood, using 40 stone steps down into a small wooded valley, then 47 stone steps to climb from it. The route cross a track, passes Griff Lodge, and enters Whinny Bank Wood. Nearby **Griff Farm** stands on the site of an old monastic grange farm associated with Rievaulx Abbey.

A clear track leads down through the woods and is scented with garlic from the abundance of ramsons growing alongside. Turn left to follow a path alongside a sunken road bend and follow the road to Rievaulx Bridge over the **River Rye**. Before crossing the bridge, consider making a detour of less than 1km (½ mile) along the road to the right to visit the impos-ing remains of **Rievaulx Abbey**. (The little village of Rievaulx might also be explored, but offers no facilities for walkers.)

map continues on page 119

Rievaulx Abbey was founded in 1132 and remains a tall and imposing edifice

117

RIEVAULX ABBEY

Founded in 1132 by Walter l'Espec, Rievaulx Abbey was a Cistercian house. During its construction a short canal was built and rafts bore blocks of stone to the site. The abbey is built almost on a north-south axis rather than the usual east-west because of its situation in a rather narrow dale. Only 35 years after its foundation the abbey boasted 140 monks, 250 lay brothers and 260 hired laymen. Even in its ruinous state the walls rise to a prodigious height and give a good impression of the size and complexity of the building. There is an entrance charge for the abbey, which also has a café and toilets, tel 01439 798228.

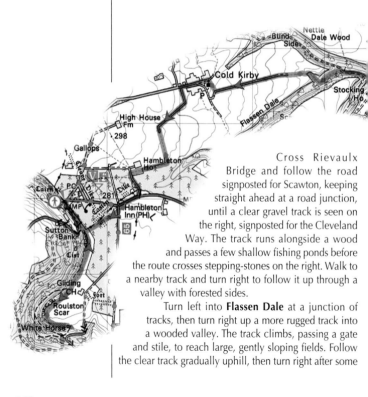

Cross Rievaulx Bridge and follow the road signposted for Scawton, keeping straight ahead at a road junction, until a clear gravel track is seen on the right, signposted for the Cleveland Way. The track runs alongside a wood and passes a few shallow fishing ponds before the route crosses stepping-stones on the right. Walk to a nearby track and turn right to follow it up through a valley with forested sides.

Turn left into **Flassen Dale** at a junction of tracks, then turn right up a more rugged track into a wooded valley. The track climbs, passing a gate and stile, to reach large, gently sloping fields. Follow the clear track gradually uphill, then turn right after some big buildings, as signposted along a path to reach the little village of **Cold Kirby**. ▸

There are no facilities in the village for walkers.

Follow the road up to the top end of the village, around 250m (820ft). Turn left as signposted, following a track through fields, then turn right, left and right again to walk alongside a forest. When a farm access road is reached near **Hambleton House** and its stables, turn left to follow it to the busy A170. Turn right and pass the **Hambleton Inn**, which is currently closed, but if it re-opens it should offer food and drink.

Walk beside the busy main road. A minor road on the left is signposted for the Yorkshire **Gliding Club**, while the Cleveland Way follows a path away from the road junction, through patchy woodland to reach a clear path on a cliff edge at 290m (950ft). A three-fingered signpost at this point might cause confusion. The Cleveland Way officially turns left, but doubles back later to pass the same path junction. The apparent detour is well worth the effort, however, as it runs around the cliffs of **Roulston Scar** to reach the very head of the Kilburn **White Horse**, enjoying wide-ranging views across the plains. ▸

Heed warning signs around the airfield. Do not short-cut across the airfield. Watch out for low-flying gliders and do not tamper with towing cables.

Limestone cliffs flank the North York Moors and drop steeply to the plains below

KILBURN WHITE HORSE

Only the head of the horse can be seen from the Cleveland Way – you need to go down to a picnic site to see much more of the beast. It was cut in 1857 under the direction of local schoolmaster John Hodgson. The inspiration came from another local man, Thomas Taylor, who had witnessed the cleaning and maintenance of a white horse carved in chalk in the south of England. As the local bedrock is oolitic limestone, rather than white chalk, the Kilburn White Horse is given occasional applications of whitewash. The figure measures 96m (314ft) by 69m (228ft) and is a landmark for many on the lower plains.

Of greater antiquity, cutting across the glider field, is the Casten Dike, which may have once formed a defensive or territorial boundary on the promontory.

Double back along the cliff path and remain on the clearest path as signposted for **Sutton Bank**. Either cross the busy A170 road to pick up the Cleveland Way on the other side, just to the left, or make a detour to the right through a car park to reach the National Park Centre. (Note that accommodation is limited to a couple of nearby farmhouse B&Bs, with no nearby campsites.)

NORTH YORK MOORS NATIONAL PARK CENTRE

The centre catches tourists at one of the busiest entry points for the national park. Displays and exhibits focus on conservation in order to encourage sensitive and thoughtful recreation. The 'Lime & Ice' exhibition focuses on the making of the landscape at Sutton Bank. Maps and guides are on sale and there is a café and toilets on site. Bicycles can be hired, and there are short walking trails available, along with supporting literature. One signpost nearby indicates the 'Finest View in England', which was much loved by the author James Herriot. For further details tel 01845 597426.

STAGE 2

Sutton Bank to Osmotherley

Start	National Park Centre, Sutton Bank (SE 515 830)
Finish	Market Cross, Osmotherley (SE 456 973)
Distance	19km (11¾ miles)
Time	6hr
Terrain	Gentle cliff-top walking on good paths, followed by a clear track over high moorland. Field paths and tracks are used towards the end.
Maps	OS Landrangers 99 and 100, OS Explorer OL26, Harvey Cleveland Way
Refreshments	Cafés at Sutton Bank National Park Centre and High Paradise Farm. Pubs and cafés at Osmotherley.
Public transport	Abbotts buses link Osmotherley with Northallerton and Stokesley, except Sunday.

This day's walk essentially traces the steep-sloping western edge of the North York Moors National Park. Although of modest altitude, never reaching as high as 400m (1300ft), views from the edge stretch far across the plains to the distant swellings of the Pennines. The Cleveland Way also begins to touch on the wilder fringes of the North York Moors, allowing walkers their first experience of the apparently endless expanses of heather moorland. The route includes part of the Hambleton Drove Road, an ancient upland thoroughfare with a long history. At the end of the day the little village of Osmotherley offers all a walker needs. Make the most of it, as there are empty stretches ahead where facilities are sparse or absent.

Leave a bend at the top of the main A170 road at **Sutton Bank**, where the Cleveland Way is signposted for Sneck Yate. The path initially runs through patchy woodland at around 300m (985ft), with only occasional glimpses over the cliffs to the left. **Gormire Lake** is seen in a wooded hollow at the foot of **Whitestone Cliff**, with agricultural plains stretching beyond.

Looking back along steep and wooded slopes to Gormire Lake and Sutton Bank

GORMIRE LAKE

This little lake is entirely natural, but unusual, since the area does not readily support lakes. It was formed when a huge section of the escarpment slumped onto the plains, the detached strata tilting back at an angle and leaving a small valley between itself and the freshly broken cliff face. The valley was filled with rubble and clay from the fracture, allowing water to pool in a hollow, when normally it would have seeped through the limestone bedrock. According to local lore the lake is bottomless, but in reality it is quite shallow. The surrounding woodlands are home to red, fallow and roe deer, although these are seldom seen.

The cliff path is grassy and gently graded, dropping slightly as it turns right and later swings left in the Garbutt Wood Nature Reserve. The cliffs become a wooded slope at **South Woods**, then there is a gradual ascent onto **Boltby Scar** where grass and bilberry, along with contorted larches, cover the site of an Iron Age hill fort at 330m (1080ft). The nearby cliff is cleft by a 'windypit' chasm which afforded a crude habitation.

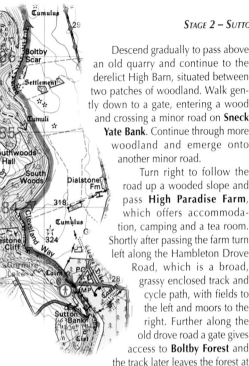

Descend gradually to pass above an old quarry and continue to the derelict High Barn, situated between two patches of woodland. Walk gently down to a gate, entering a wood and crossing a minor road on **Sneck Yate Bank**. Continue through more woodland and emerge onto another minor road.

Turn right to follow the road up a wooded slope and pass **High Paradise Farm**, which offers accommodation, camping and a tea room. Shortly after passing the farm turn left along the Hambleton Drove Road, which is a broad, grassy enclosed track and cycle path, with fields to the left and moors to the right. Further along the old drove road a gate gives access to **Boltby Forest** and the track later leaves the forest at another gate at **Steeple Cross**. ▶

map continues on page 124

This might not have been a true wayside cross, but a marker for routes branching from the drove road.

HAMBLETON DROVE ROAD

No doubt this ancient road was based on a prehistoric ridgeway route. Travellers and traders preferred to keep to the high ground rather than risk passage through the plains, which were once densely wooded, swampy in places, and inhabited by wild animals. Even long after the lowlands were tamed, drovers moving livestock from Scotland to London used the high ground to avoid enclosed farmland and expensive turnpikes. Covering immense distances, drovers could get a good price when stock was scarce around the capital. The 18th and 19th centuries saw brisk trade, with herds of up to a thousand animals on the move. As drovers could be charged 1s/6d (7.5 pence) per score of cattle to use a turnpike, great savings were made by avoiding them altogether.

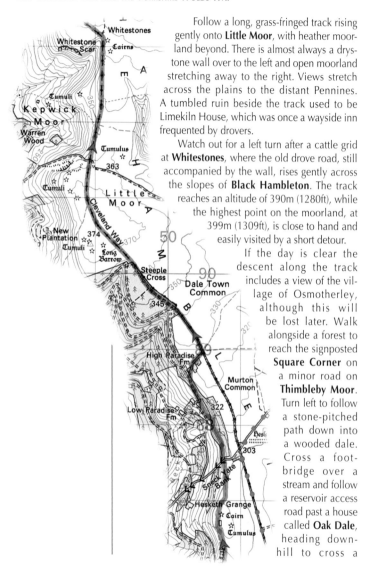

Follow a long, grass-fringed track rising gently onto **Little Moor**, with heather moorland beyond. There is almost always a drystone wall over to the left and open moorland stretching away to the right. Views stretch across the plains to the distant Pennines. A tumbled ruin beside the track used to be Limekiln House, which was once a wayside inn frequented by drovers.

Watch out for a left turn after a cattle grid at **Whitestones**, where the old drove road, still accompanied by the wall, rises gently across the slopes of **Black Hambleton**. The track reaches an altitude of 390m (1280ft), while the highest point on the moorland, at 399m (1309ft), is close to hand and easily visited by a short detour.

If the day is clear the descent along the track includes a view of the village of Osmotherley, although this will be lost later. Walk alongside a forest to reach the signposted **Square Corner** on a minor road on **Thimbleby Moor**. Turn left to follow a stone-pitched path down into a wooded dale. Cross a footbridge over a stream and follow a reservoir access road past a house called **Oak Dale**, heading downhill to cross a bridge before climbing uphill through woods.

Turn left down a minor road, then right up a track. Turn left downhill, towards **Whitehouse Farm**, but keep well to the right along a path and walk down to a footbridge spanning a stream. Climb steps on a wooded slope and follow a clear path through fields to reach the village of **Osmotherley**. Simply walk straight ahead, quietly, along a narrow alleyway to reach the Market Cross on a green in the middle of the village.

OSMOTHERLEY

This is a charming stone village with a green heart. Three roads meet at the Market Cross and nearby is a stone table on five legs where baskets of market produce were sold. John Wesley preached from this table, and the Methodist chapel in the village bears a date-stone of 1754.

Facilities in the village include a handful of accommodation options, from a hotel to bed-and-breakfasts. The youth hostel and campsite are just outside the village – walk up North End to reach them. There is a post office, a pub and a few shops. Abbotts buses run through the village, linking with Northallerton and Stokesley, except Sunday.

STAGE 3

Osmotherley to Clay Bank

Start	Market Cross, Osmotherley (SE 456 973)
Finish	B1257, Clay Bank (NZ 573 033)
Distance	17.5km (11 miles)
Time	5hr 15min
Terrain	A series of forest walks, hill climbs and exposed high moorlands. Some paths are quite steep and rugged.
Maps	OS Landrangers 93 and 99, OS Explorer OL26, Harvey Cleveland Way
Refreshments	Pub off-route at Swainby. Café at Lord Stones. Possible snack van at Clay Bank.
Public transport	Abbotts buses link Osmotherley with Northallerton and Stokesley, except Sunday. Summer weekend Moorsbus services cross Clay Bank, between Chop Gate and Great Broughton. With advance notice, nearby accommodation providers usually offer pick-ups and drop-offs.

This part of the Cleveland Way is remarkably hilly, rather like a monstrous roller coaster. On a clear day, with time to enjoy the surroundings, it is also a very scenic and enjoyable stretch, but in foul weather there is little shelter from the elements and the sight of yet another steep climb can be dispiriting. While strong walkers could combine this with the next day's walk to Kildale, the total distance and the effort involved would be daunting for some. Breaking the journey at Clay Bank means that you have to follow the road one way or the other, to Great Broughton or Chop Gate, to reach accommodation. Summer weekend Moorsbus services could be used, otherwise most of the nearby accommodation providers offer pick-ups and drop-offs, but be sure to check that these will be available when booking. There is a good mobile phone signal at Clay Bank, for when it is time to call for a lift.

Leave **Osmotherley** by following the road called North End. Pass a pinfold, where stray animals were once impounded. Turn left near the top of the village as sign-posted for the Cleveland Way, along Ruebury Lane. Follow this access road as it climbs past a few houses, continuing uphill along a track to reach a fork. The **Lady Chapel** is signposted up to the right and is worth a short detour, but the Cleveland Way is signposted to the left, running close to **Chapel Wood Farm**.

LADY CHAPEL AND MOUNT GRACE PRIORY

Lady Chapel is attached to a house and is said to have been built by Catherine of Aragon, first wife of Henry VIII, in 1515 for the recluse Thomas Parkinson. A number of miracles are said to have taken place there and the chapel remains a popular site of pilgrimage, being reached by a track lined with the Stations of the Cross.

Off-route, but worthy of note, is Mount Grace Priory, reached by detouring downhill through Arncliffe Wood. This was a Carthusian monastery founded in 1398 by Thomas de Holand. Of particular interest are the two-storey monk's cells around the cloister, one of which has been restored to its original condition. Each cell had a living room, study, bedroom and small herb garden. The central tower of the priory church remains intact. The site is generally open at weekends and there is an entrance charge, tel 01609 883494.

Keep straight along the track, through a gate and away from Chapel Wood Farm, to reach a gate into **Arncliffe Wood**. Turn right up a clear path, also used by the Coast to Coast Walk, and continue along the inside edge of the wood, following a drystone wall over the crest of the hill.

Pass the British Telecom station on Beacon Hill, as well as a trig point at 299m (981ft), then drop downhill to reach a couple of gates leading onto heathery **Scarth Wood Moor**. ▶ Bear in mind that for the rest of the day the Coast to Coast Walk and Lyke Wake Walk run along the same course as the Cleveland Way. A clear, paved path runs down the moorland slope, then a left turn leads down a steeper pitched path to reach a minor road at **Scarth Nick**.

Views ahead take in the hilly parts of the Cleveland Way with the little pyramidal peak of Roseberry Topping seen in the distance.

127

A stagnant mass of ice melting on higher ground caused a torrent of glacial melt-water to pour through a gap in the hills, cutting **Scarth Nick**. The road at Scarth Nick is steep but otherwise innocuous. However, in the 18th century the well-travelled Arthur Young was scathing about it, saying, 'The going down into Cleveland is beyond all description terrible… for you go through such steep, rough, narrow, rocky precipices that I would sincerely advise any friend to go a hundred miles to avoid it.'

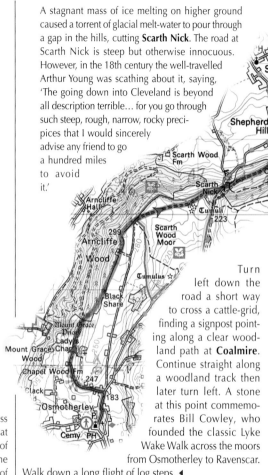

Turn left down the road a short way to cross a cattle-grid, finding a signpost pointing along a clear woodland path at **Coalmire**. Continue straight along a woodland track then later turn left. A stone at this point commemorates Bill Cowley, who founded the classic Lyke Wake Walk across the moors from Osmotherley to Ravenscar. Walk down a long flight of log steps. ◄

Turn right without going through the gate to stay inside the wood, enjoying the sight of huge oak trees. Watch for a left turn later, which leads out of the wood and down through a field. Follow a track to cross a foot-bridge or ford a river, then turn left to follow a road across

There is access through a gate at the bottom end of the wood to the nearby village of Swainby, where facilities include Blacksmiths Arms, Black Horse Inn and Rusty Bike Café.

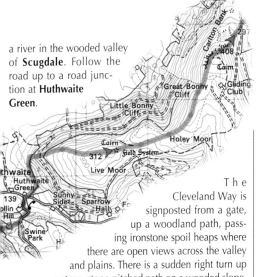

a river in the wooded valley of **Scugdale**. Follow the road up to a road junction at **Huthwaite Green**.

map continues on page 130

The Cleveland Way is signposted from a gate, up a woodland path, passing ironstone spoil heaps where there are open views across the valley and plains. There is a sudden right turn up a steep, stone-pitched path on a wooded slope, then continue climbing less steeply up a stone-paved moorland path. This levels out as it crosses the 312m (1024ft) summit of **Live Moor**, where views stretch around the North York Moors.

Cross a broad and heathery dip in the moorland then climb again on **Holey Moor**, passing alongside a former gliding club field, now overgrown. A trig point is reached at 408m (1338ft) alongside a stone upright on **Carlton Moor**. ▶ Follow a stone-paved path steeply down to a gap, passing close to a quarried edge protected by a fence. Cross a track and a road on the lower slopes of **Carlton Bank**.

Enjoy splendid views across the plains, from the distant Pennines to industrial Teesdale, past the little peak of Roseberry Topping, around the North York Moors and back along the Cleveland Way in the direction of Osmotherley.

ALTERNATIVE ROUTE BETWEEN CARLTON BANK AND CLAY BANK

Those contemplating this walk on a day of foul weather should bear in mind that there are paths and tracks cutting across the northern slopes of the hills between Carlton Bank and Clay Bank. The first part of this low-level route is known as the Miners' Track and is then followed by forest tracks. The miners worked these slopes for alum, jet and ironstone.

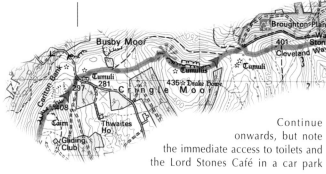

Continue
onwards, but note
the immediate access to toilets and
the Lord Stones Café in a car park

*The view back along
the way from Cringle
End to Lord Stones
and Carlton Bank*

surrounded by trees. (Camping is available in the **Country Park**, but ask first at the café.) ▶ Walk across a grassy common to leave the café, then follow a grassy track flanked by a fence and drystone wall. Go through a gate and continue up a paved path close to the wall. A stone viewpoint seat dedicated to local rambler Alec Falconer is reached at **Cringle End**. Climb higher along a gritty path and a paved path along the top of the abrupt northern edge of **Cringle Moor**, around 420m (1380ft).

A steep, winding, stone-pitched path leads downhill, passing alum shale spoil before reaching a fork at a gap. Keep right at the fork to go through a gate, then follow another steep, stone-pitched path over the top of **Cold Moor** at 401m (1316ft). Drop down to another gate and another grassy gap.

The next steep climb passes to the left of jagged, blocky **Wain Stones**, which are worth studying from all angles, and are completely out of character with the

The road can be used to reach Carlton, 2.5km (1½ miles) off-route, for a pub, or West Cote and Chop Gate, 4 to 5.5km (2½ to 3½ miles) off-route, for accommodation and a pub.

The Wain Stones are popular with rock-climbers and photographers

131

A snack van might be available at a nearby forest car park on the Great Broughton side of the gap, but don't rely on it being there.

smooth contours prevalent around the North York Moors. Some hands-on scrambling is required, then once above them, a delightful level path runs along a moorland edge at 390m (1280ft) on **Hasty Bank**. At the end of this lofty promenade a steep path runs downhill, later following a wall. Some 60 stone steps complete the descent to the B1257 road at **Clay Bank**. ◀

Reaching the road on **Clay Bank** is not strictly the end of the day's walk. Strong walkers may well cross the road and continue to Kildale, while others will have booked accommodation in **Great Broughton** to the north or **Chop Gate** to the south. These are the two nearest villages, located in opposite directions, 4km (2½ miles) off-route. To avoid walking the additional distance, either use summer weekend Moorsbus services, or ask in advance if accommodation providers are willing to provide pick-ups and drop-offs.

CHOP GATE

The hamlet of Chop Gate is located 4km (2½ miles) down the road in Bilsdale. Facilities are limited to the Buck Inn, offering food, drink, accommodation and camping.

GREAT BROUGHTON

The village of Great Broughton is located on the plains. The Wainstones Hotel offers food, drink and accommodation, and there are other lodgings nearby, as well as a campsite. There are a couple of pubs and The Little Shop. Abbotts buses link Great Broughton with Stokesley, Osmotherley and Northallerton.

STAGE 4
Clay Bank to Kildale

Start	B1257, Clay Bank (NZ 573 033)
Finish	Glebe Cottage, Kildale (NZ 607 094)
Distance	15km (9½ miles)
Time	5hr
Terrain	High and exposed moorlands, but good paths and tracks. Care is needed with route-finding in poor visibility.
Maps	OS Landrangers 93 and 94, OS Explorer OL26, Harvey Cleveland Way
Refreshment	None along the route, then limited to a tea garden at Kildale.
Public transport	Kildale is served by daily Northern trains linking Middlesbrough and Whitby.

This is the most remote part of the Cleveland Way, traversing the highest part of the North York Moors, with no easy access to facilities of any kind. Accommodation, food and drink are limited even at the end of the day around Kildale. Walkers who cannot secure lodgings in Kildale, and who don't wish to cover any more of the route during the day, should check the times of trains passing through the village. These link with nearby villages and even distant towns such as Whitby and Middlesbrough. In foul weather walkers need to keep a careful eye on their maps. Paths and tracks are generally clear, but a wrong turning could involve a huge detour. In calm, clear weather this is one of the most memorable parts of the route, especially when the heather moorlands are flushed purple in the summer.

Leave the B1257 road at **Clay Bank** and follow a steep, stone-pitched path uphill alongside a wall. Go through small gates, then at the top of the slope the path runs at a gentler gradient across the higher moorlands. The broad crest is called Carr Ridge and it rises to around 380m (1250ft). There are views back to the hilly parts of the Cleveland Way, but now the terrain, although remote and exposed, is gentler. The path is mostly gritty, with grass, heather or bilberry alongside, although a few short stretches are paved with stone.

Keep left at a junction, in effect straight ahead, roughly along the crest of **Urra Moor**, passing close to a trig point. This actually sits on a burial mound on **Round Hill** at 454m (1490ft). It can be reached by a short diversion along a path on the left, and it is the highest point on the moors, as well as in the whole of this guidebook! ◄

Note the Hand Stone and Face Stone beside the track, which are old route markers on the moor.

The trig point on **Round Hill** sits on the squat remains of a moorland burial mound. The North York Moors are dotted with similar mounds, and some parts are criss-crossed by ancient earthworks that were either territorial markers or defensive structures. The moorland marker stones are of more recent antiquity, dating from around the 18th century. The Hand Stone has two open palms, bearing the words, 'This way to Stoxla' (Stokesley) and 'This way to Kirbie'

map continues on page 137

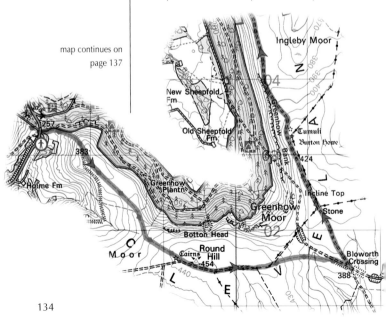

(Kirkbymoorside). The older Face Stone features a crudely carved face.

Continue along the clearest track and later pass a junction with another track, keeping straight ahead. When the track suddenly turns left, leave it by following a path on the right. This runs down a moorland slope and is partly stone-paved, climbing a short way to join the old trackbed of the Rosedale Railway. Turn right to pass a barrier gate and reach a signposted intersection of tracks at **Bloworth Crossing**, around 400m (1310ft).

Looking back towards Clay Bank while climbing onto the broad Urra Moor

ROSEDALE MINERAL RAILWAY

The railway operated from 1861 to 1929, during which time it transported iron ore from Rosedale to the blast furnaces of Durham. The line contoured along the upper slopes of Rosedale and Farndale, as high as 410m (1345ft), before reaching a sudden 20% (1 in 5) incline on Greenhow Bank. Cottages at the top of the incline were known as Siberia by the workers, owing to their remoteness. Loaded wagons were lowered three at a time from a winding house, while empty wagons were drawn back up the line. The remote Bloworth Crossing was manned by a keeper at a time when the old road over the moor carried more traffic than it does today. The keeper lived beside the level crossing in a lonely house, which has long been demolished.

The Coast to Coast Walk and Lyke Wake Walk continue along the railway trackbed. They won't be seen again until they finish at Robin Hood's Bay and Ravenscar.

The Cleveland Way turns sharp left, rising gently along another broad, clear track. ◄ The stony track passes a pair of upright **stones**. The taller of these is relatively modern, dated 1888, while the shorter one is considerably older and is known as Jenny Bradley's Cross. The high moorland track seems to run on forever when seen from **Greenhow Bank**. Look out for the Guide Stone away to the right.

Jenny Bradley sounds like the name of a person, but 'Bradley' is thought to derive from 'Broad Ley', or a broad trackway. **Jenny Bradley's Cross** is a little stump of a stone cross that merely marks an old track over the moors, and the taller stone is a 19th-century boundary stone between moorland estates.

The 18th-century **Guide Stone** is easily missed in poor visibility, lying further away from the track. It offers the following directions: 'Ingleby and Stoxley' (Stokesley), 'Kirby (Kirkbymoorside) and Helmsley', and 'Gisbro' (Guisborough). Of interest to cash-strapped walkers is a hollow on top of the stone that usually contains a few coins. From

Jenny Bradley's Cross stands beside a taller stone pillar near Bloworth Crossing

1711 it was a requirement that signposts and guide-stones were erected on routes such as this, although naturally the stone markers outlived the wooden ones.

Keep walking northwards along the track, across **Ingleby Moor**, until another track signposted for the Cleveland Way branches off to the right at a gate. This track leads along another moorland crest over **Battersby Moor**. Keep straight ahead at a track junction, eventually reaching a gate at a bend on a minor road. Follow the road straight ahead, cross a rise on **Kildale Moor** at 335m (1100ft), and turn left at a corner to cross a cattle grid. The road passes a memorial to a crashed aircraft, then runs down and around the slopes of Park Nab to reach a broad and green valley. When a road junction is reached, turn right for **Kildale** and later turn left for Glebe Cottage.

Horse-riders enjoy following the high track across Battersby Moor above Kildale

KILDALE

This small village has only limited facilities, including camping and a camping barn at Low Farm, a tearoom at Glebe Cottage, and a couple of nearby B&Bs. If lodgings cannot be secured within walking distance, then go down to the railway station where daily Northern train services allow nearby villages, or the more distant towns of Whitby and Middlesbrough, to be reached. There are toilets at the railway station.

STAGE 5
Kildale to Saltburn-by-the-Sea

Start	Glebe Cottage, Kildale (NZ 607 094)
Finish	The Zetland, Saltburn-by-the-Sea (NZ 665 214)
Distance	24km (15 miles)
Time	7hr 30min
Terrain	Forest and moorland tracks are generally clear, but care is needed at junctions. Easy field paths give way to suburban walking on pavements.
Maps	OS Landrangers 93 and 94, OS Explorer OL26, Harvey Cleveland Way
Refreshments	Pub at Slapewath. Pubs at Skelton Green and Skelton. Plenty of pubs, cafés and restaurants at Saltburn.
Public transport	Kildale is served by daily Northern trains linking Middlesbrough and Whitby. Arriva buses link Slapewath, near Guisborough, with Middlesbrough, Whitby, Robin Hood's Bay and Scarborough. Arriva buses also serve Skelton and Saltburn-by-the-Sea. Arriva buses and Northern trains link Saltburn-by-the-Sea with Middlesbrough.

The Cleveland Way enters Captain Cook Country, visiting Captain Cook's Monument on Easby Moor. Roseberry Topping has occasionally been in view during the previous couple of days. Walkers now come face to face with it, and while many choose to climb it, others omit it. An ascent is part of the 'official' route, but it does represent extra effort and a retracing of steps. The bustling town of Guisborough can be seen, but the route passes high above it through Guisborough Forest. The North York Moors National Park is left behind for a while at Slapewath, and the route wanders through Skelton to reach Saltburn-by-the-Sea. After remote moorland days with sparse facilities, the trail reaches the cliff coast where accommodation options abound and food and drink are plentiful.

Starting from Glebe Cottage in **Kildale**, walk down the road signposted as the Cleveland Way. Follow the road under the railway, cross the **River Leven** and climb past **Bankside Farm**. Turn left at the top of the road to follow a forest track along the crest of **Coate Moor**. Branch left along a gravel forest path signposted for the Cleveland Way. Walk straight through the woods then climb up a paved path. Continue through a gap in a wall onto the heathery **Easby Moor**. Walk straight towards a prominent stone obelisk, which is **Captain Cook's Monument**, standing at 324m (1063ft).

Captain Cook's Monument, erected on Easby Moor, is a prominent landmark

CAPTAIN COOK'S MONUMENT

This fine stone obelisk stands 15m (51ft) high and overlooks Marton, the suburb of Middlesbrough where James Cook was born in 1728, and Great Ayton, where he received an education from 1736 to 1740. Cook's father was employed at Airy Holme Farm, where Mr Scottowe paid for James' education at the Michael Postgate School, which is now the Captain Cook Schoolroom Museum. The inscription on the obelisk reads, 'In memory of Captain Cook the celebrated navigator. A man in nautical knowledge inferior to none. In zeal, prudence and energy superior to most. Regardless of the danger he opened an intercourse with the Friendly Isles and other parts of the Southern Hemisphere. Born at Marton in 1728. Massacred at Owhyee (Hawaii) 1779.'

Follow a stone-paved path away from the monument, pass a memorial to a crashed aircraft, and walk down a path and track on a forested slope. Turn right along a minor

road, then almost immediately turn left up a flight of 115 steps. The gradient eases on **Great Ayton Moor**, where there is a wall and a clear-felled forest to the left and open heather moorland to the right. Simply follow a clear track onwards, around

map continues on page 143

View of Roseberry Topping's distinctive outline on the descent from Easby Moor

290m (950ft), with the wall always to the left. The wall suddenly turns a corner on **Newton Moor** where a gate gives access to **Roseberry Topping**.

Quarried and scarred, undermined for ironstone, leading to partial collapse in 1907, **Roseberry Topping** has suffered greatly through the years but has by no means been diminished. The 'Yorkshire Matterhorn' bears its scars proudly and presents an aggressive face to the plains. The detour to the summit is an 'official' part of the Cleveland Way, but some walkers take one look and decide they can do without the exercise on its admittedly steep slopes. Climb it or don't climb it – the choice is yours. Omitting it will save 2km (1¼ miles) from the day's walk, but it may always irk you later!

Go through the gate if you wish to climb Roseberry Topping. The path is paved as it drops steeply downhill, levelling out on a grassy gap. Another stone-paved path winds steeply up the rugged slopes of Roseberry Topping to reach bare sandstone slabs and a trig point at 320m (1050ft). Enjoy the views from this airy perch, looking out across the plains to the distant Pennines and industrial Teesmouth, as well as to the nearby North York Moors. Retrace steps back across the gap to return to the gate in the corner of the wall on **Newton Moor**.

Walk along a clear, gravel path that cuts straight across the heather moorland. Go through a small gate and turn right to follow a track between a clear-felled forest and a fence. Pass a barrier gate at a junction of tracks and then turn right through another gate to leave the forest, following a track up a moorland slope for a short way. Watch for a stone-paved path heading off to the left, running down into a dip in the moorland, then walk uphill alongside a wall with **Highcliffe Farm** only a couple of fields away to the left. ▸ Pass through a kissing gate and later turn left through another kissing gate, as signposted for the Cleveland Way. Walk past a stand of beech trees.

The stone slabs include two halves of a broken dedication stone from Holy Trinity School, Halifax.

Walk down a path and swing right, climbing across a track as signposted. Pass a worn path, then turn right up a stone-pitched path. Climb alongside an old quarry on **Highcliff Nab**, then turn left along the top edge of the quarry, where there is a fine view over the busy little town of Guisborough. Follow a track onwards through the forest then fork left at a junction of tracks, dropping steeply. Keep walking straight ahead through **Guisborough Woods**, but watch for a sudden turn uphill to the right. Though steep, the route soon levels out and walkers simply keep straight ahead

map continues on page 145

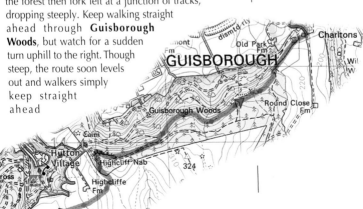

143

again, more or less level. Go straight through an intersection of tracks, keep an eye on marker posts at junctions, and later there is a turn down to the left, running alongside the forest.

Watch for a gate on the right to follow a path out of the forest, then turn left down a concrete road on a wooded slope. Turn right at a cattle-grid to walk along the lower edge of the wood. Keep off a broad, bare terrace of crushed alum-shale spoil and instead follow a path beside a woodland fence as marked and signposted for the Cleveland Way. Keep an eye on directional arrow markers, basically contouring across a wooded slope before turning left down to the busy main A171. Turn left alongside the main road, then turn right to cross the main road to reach **Slapewath**, where the Fox and Hound offers food, drink and accommodation.

Guisborough can be seen from Highcliff Nab, but lies off-route

Guisborough attracts the attention of walkers, but lies off-route. It can be reached easily enough either by making a detour on foot or by catching a bus from Slapewath. The cobbled High Street is full of character, but the town's centrepiece is Gisborough

Priory. This was an Augustinian house, founded in 1119 by Robert de Brus, but rebuilt after being destroyed by a fire in 1289. There is an entrance charge, tel 01287 633801. Also of interest are the Guisborough Museum on Westgate, tel 01287 203617, and the nearby Guisborough Forest and Walkway Visitor Centre, tel 01287 631132.

Facilities in Guisborough include accommodation, banks with ATMs, a post office, toilets, plenty of pubs, internationally flavoured restaurants and shops. Regular Arriva bus services run from Guisborough or Slapewath to Middlesbrough, as well as to Whitby, Robin Hood's Bay and Scarborough.

Walk away from the Fox and Hound to nearby cottages, where a path rises to an old quarry. Keep to the right-hand side of the quarry, climbing almost 200 wooden steps up a slope of gorse bushes. When the upper edge of the quarry is reached, climb straight uphill, then turn right to continue uphill beside a field. A track leads past **Airy Hill Farm** to reach the little village of **Skelton Green**. Walk along Airy Hill Lane to reach a road junction near the Green

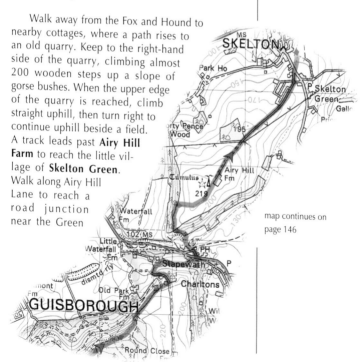

map continues on page 146

SALTBURN-BY-THE-SEA

Inn, where there are bus services.

Cross the road and follow a tarmac path onwards through fields. There is a view towards Skelton Castle before dropping down to a narrow road. Turn right along the road then left down a flight of 90 steps into **Skelton**. Cross the busy A173 road, or High Street, and continue straight ahead. Turn right along Derwent Road, beside a library, and follow this suburban road as it bends left downhill. Go through a crossroads and later turn right at the bottom, into a field as signposted. Veer left on entering the field, then turn left to walk straight past a housing development. Cross a road and walk straight onwards, then turn right in a wooded area and go beneath the A174 by-pass.

Skelton Green is a small village with a couple of pubs available for thirsty walkers, as well as bus services to and from Saltburn-by-the-Sea and Middlesbrough. **Skelton** is a larger and busier village with the same bus services, as well as a post office, accommodation, a couple more pubs, cafés, takeaways and a variety of shops.

A clear woodland path leads downhill, using steps and turning a sharp bend to reach **Skelton Beck**. Cross a footbridge and go beneath a towering arch, one of 11 supporting the monumental brick-built Saltburn Viaduct, in use since 1872. Keep an eye on marker posts at path junctions, passing a notice for the Saltburn Valley Gardens. Stay on woodland paths, catching the garlic scent of ramsons, until signposts indicate the way to the town centre.

Go up a few steps on the road called Albion Terrace in **Saltburn-by-the-Sea**. Turn right along the road and follow it until it passes between The Zetland, formerly a prominent hotel, and the Spa Hotel. Alternatively, walk into the town centre to avail of its full range of services.

SALTBURN-BY-THE-SEA

Saltburn was originally no more than a huddle of cottages at the foot of the cliffs. The old village had a history of smuggling, where John Andrew was known as 'the king of the smugglers'. The opening of a railway in 1861 transformed the place, and the elegant new town built on top of the cliffs was a quintessential Victorian spa resort. In 1869 a pier stretching 450m (1500ft) out to sea was constructed, but it has been damaged on a number of occasions by storm and shipwreck and is rather shorter these days. A hydraulic cliff lift was built in 1884 to spare people trudging up and down the steep slope between the town and the beach. Like many old seaside resorts Saltburn's grandeur has faded, but it remains an interesting place and walkers will find it offers much after the lonely moors.

Facilities in Saltburn include a good range of accommodation, banks with ATMs, a post office, toilets, plenty of pubs, restaurants and tearooms, as well as a splendid range of shops. Arriva buses run from Saltburn to Middlesbrough, as well as along the coast to Whitby. Northern trains run daily to and from Middlesbrough.

A cliff lift serves a pier in the Victorian resort of Saltburn

STAGE 6

Saltburn-by-the-Sea to Sandsend

Start	The Zetland, Saltburn-by-the-Sea (NZ 665 214)
Finish	Sandsend (NZ 860 129)
Distance	27.5km (17 miles)
Time	8hr 30min
Terrain	Cliff coast walking involving some steep ascents and descents. Parts of the route use field paths set back from the cliff. Village streets require careful route-finding. High tides at Runswick Bay can cover a short beach walk.
Maps	OS Landranger 94, OS Explorers OL26 and OL27, Harvey Cleveland Way
Refreshments	Pub and take-away at Skinningrove. Several pubs and cafés at Staithes. Restaurant off-route at Port Mulgrave. Pubs and a beach café at Runswick Bay. Pubs and restaurants at Sandsend.
Public transport	Arriva buses link Saltburn with Middlesbrough and Skinningrove. Arriva buses also link Staithes, Runswick Bay and Sandsend with Middlesbrough and Whitby.

The Cleveland Way enjoys its first day along the coast, taking in splendid cliffs and coves. After leaving Saltburn the route traverses Hunt Cliff to reach industrial Skinningrove, then climbs over Boulby Cliff, which is the highest cliff on the east coast of England, to descend to the charming and colourful harbour village of Staithes. This is where the young James Cook worked as a shopkeeper's assistant and was inspired by the comings and goings of seafarers to consider a change of career. The Captain Cook and Staithes Heritage Centre offers plenty of background information. The cliff coast continues to Runswick Bay, a lovely little village on a steep slope facing a bay fringed by golden sands. This might be far enough for some walkers, but it is worth continuing to Sandsend to finish just short of Whitby, so that this old whaling town can be explored early the following morning.

Leave **Saltburn-by-the-Sea** by following the Marine Parade from The Zetland to the top of the Cliff Lift. Walk

Walkers climb steeply from Skinningrove, with Hunt Cliff seen in the far distance

down a path featuring 75 concrete steps to reach a road bend near the beach at **Saltburn Sands**. Cross a footbridge beside a road bridge over a river, and follow the road past boats and rusty tractors to reach The Ship. ▶

Climb 90 steps behind the pub to reach a grassy cliff top, passing a marker stone for the Cleveland Heritage Coast, and later passing a sign for the Hunt Cliff Nature Reserve. **Hunt Cliff** has plenty of ledges where fulmars and kittiwakes nest, while cormorants are also commonly observed. The grasslands along the cliff tops are one of the few places in the country where 'dyer's greenweed' grows. The flowers of this small shrub yield a yellow dye which used to be mixed with woad to create the colour 'Kendal green'.

This was once the haunt of smugglers.

In recent years the site of a **Roman signal station** was passed on Hunt Cliff, but it has been lost over the cliff edge. It was probably constructed around 367AD, and may have been attacked and its occupants slain, as 14 bodies were found dumped in an adjacent well when the site was excavated. The station was linked by line of sight with other stations along the coast at Goldsborough, Ravenscar, Scarborough, Filey Brigg and Flamborough Head – each one intended to keep a lookout for seaborne invaders.

The 'cliff' above is actually formed of slag from the steelworks, dumped in a molten state, where it rapidly solidified.

At over 100m (330ft) above sea level the path finds itself hemmed in between the cliffs and a railway line which serves a steelworks at Skinningrove and the Boulby Potash Mine. A couple of intriguing ironwork sculptures stand beside the path and there are good views both ways along the coast. Walk gradually downhill, then turn left down several flights of steps to reach a sandy path running past dunes spiked with marram grass. ◄

Go through a gap in a concrete jetty and walk round the tiny harbour at **Skinningrove**, passing the 'Repus' – a traditional fishing coble now serving as a monument. Cross a bridge to reach a small boatyard with tractors.

The industrial village of **Skinningrove** looks a little down-at-heel, with some houses standing empty, while allotment huts and pigeon lofts look rather huddled and forlorn. It was no more than a quiet fishing cove until 1850, but it was transformed once the local ironstone began to be worked and a thriving steelworks was built. It became known as 'the valley of iron'. The steelworks survives as a shadow of its former self, yet it occupies a site as big as the village.

A short detour inland, signposted for the Riverside Building, reveals a fish and chip shop, post office/shop, a pub, guest house, café/bar and the Cleveland Ironstone Mining Museum, tel 01287 642877. Arriva buses link with Saltburn and Middlesbrough.

A steep and arduous stone-pitched path climbs from Skinningrove onto **Hummersea Cliff**. The path levels out on the grassy cliff-top around 70m (230ft) and the village is soon lost to sight. Hummersea Beach can

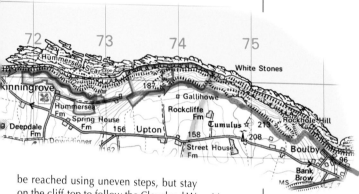

be reached using uneven steps, but stay on the cliff-top to follow the Cleveland Way. Move uphill and inland to a track, then turn left to walk up to a farm at end of the track. Go through a gate above the buildings, as signposted, and rise gradually along a narrow path across a slope covered in gorse bushes, going through a couple of kissing gates and crossing small duckboards.

map continues on page 152

Walk between the cliff edge and fields at **Gallihowe**, overlooking the extensive Loftus Alum Quarries. ▶ Enjoy extensive views ahead along the coastal path and back along the course of the Cleveland Way towards Guisborough Forest, with the North York Moors beyond. The North York Moors National Park is entered again as the route climbs onto the highest part of the cliffs, around 200m (655ft) above sea level.

Take care near the cliff edge and beware of deep fissures.

By the time the old alum quarries are passed the path is already descending. Turn left downhill to avoid walking through fields ahead, then turn right around the corner of

View along the coast from Boulby Cliff, the highest cliff on England's east coast

a fence to continue along the lower cliffs, passing a row of former alum workers' cottages at **Boulby**. Walk down a narrow road to Boulby Lodge then continue straight along a grassy path through the fields. The **Boulby Mine** can be seen inland.

BOULBY MINE

This is the only potash and polyhalite mine in the country. It has been operating since 1973 and at the time of writing hopes to produce more than a million tonnes per year, but the mineral is not easily won. The shafts drop to a depth of 1500m (4900ft) and run 7km (4½ miles) out beneath the North Sea, deeper than any other mine in the country. An extension to the mine was granted permission in 2015. The beds being mined were deposited from an extremely saline, landlocked sea in the Permian period, around 230 million years ago. Most of the mining is done by remote control, temperatures being above 40°C even before the machines start cutting, despite cooling from a powerful ventilation system. The roof of the mine has to be preserved at all costs, since a breach would allow overlying soft marl to 'flow' into the mine under pressure. Potash and polyhalite have many uses in the chemical industry, but are chiefly used for agricultural fertiliser. Rock salt is also mined at the site.

The path from Boulby Lodge reaches a crumbling cliff edge, so walk along the road, which has itself been moved inland on occasions. The road closest to the cliff is barred to traffic and leads to a junction with the more recent road further inland. Turn left down to the

charming, colourful village of **Staithes**. Cross a footbridge over the narrow harbour to reach the main part of the village.

The narrow, crooked, natural harbour, with its protective projecting cliff face at Cowbar Nab, made **Staithes** an ideal retreat for fishermen, traders and smugglers. The higgledy-piggledy houses and narrow alleys have enchanted artists and photographers for decades. For a thorough grounding in the history of this delightfully jumbled village, be sure to visit the Captain Cook and Staithes Heritage Centre, tel 01947 841454. The teenage James Cook worked as an assistant to a shopkeeper called William Sanderson in Staithes. The sea destroyed the original shop, but parts of it were incorporated into Captain

map continues on page 156

153

The charming, huddled village of Staithes sits in a narrow, natural tidal inlet

Cook's Cottage. Cook stayed only for 18 months, then moved to Whitby to train as an apprentice seaman and embark on his seafaring career.

Facilities in Staithes include a little accommodation, a campsite, post office, toilets, a few pubs, cafés, takeaways and shops. Arriva buses run from Staithes Lane End back to Saltburn and Middlesbrough, and ahead to Runswick Bay, Sandsend and Whitby.

After crossing the footbridge over the harbour at Staithes, walk up to a narrow, cobbled street and turn left. The pub called the Cod & Lobster is reached, which has been partially demolished by storms three times. Turn right up Church Street and pass Captain Cook's Cottage. Follow the stone-paved Cleveland Way even further uphill to leave the village, taking a last fond look back at the intriguing jumble of cottages.

Turn left, as signposted for Runswick Bay, to follow a clear path past a farm. Turn left as signposted along a broad grassy track flanked by fences. Turn right along the cliff tops and right again above the promontory of **Old Nab**, climbing steadily. Keep climbing, almost to 100m (330ft) on Beacon Hill. The next road, Rosedale Lane, could be followed inland from **Port Mulgrave** to reach Restaurant Number 20; otherwise stay on the route. ▶

Hinderwell, further inland, offers a couple more pubs, fish and chips, post office/shop, accommodation, campsite and bus services.

Although the broken remains of a small harbour can be seen at **Port Mulgrave**, access from the tiny village is restricted. In fact access to the harbour lies through underground tunnels originating far inland at the Grinkle ironstone mines, so there was no need for a road link from the village. Ironstone was later removed from Grinkle by rail, and as the tunnels were no longer needed they were closed, leaving the harbour unused by 1916.

The Cleveland Way is signposted off a corner of the road and along the top of the rugged slope known as Rosedale Cliffs. Go down and up flights of steps, then follow the path around **Lingrow Howe**, eventually reaching a small pond, then turn right inland to reach the Runswick Bay Hotel at Runswick Bank Top. Turn left along the road to pass the Cliffemount Hotel and walk down a narrow road closed to vehicles. Continue down to the beach at **Runswick Bay**.

The delightful little village of **Runswick Bay** is stacked up a steep slope facing a curved bay with a fine sandy beach. Despite its obvious beauty the

situation looks precarious. One night in 1664, when most of the villagers were attending a funeral wake, the houses started to slip into the sea. By morning every dwelling was in ruins, except, for some mysterious reason, the house of the dead man. Some claim that this house is the one now known as Jubilee Cottage. A sea wall protects the current village from landslip. A thatched cottage was formerly inhabited by the coastguard, who would have had one of the best vantage points to observe all the comings and goings around the bay.

Facilities around Runswick Bay include a few hotels, bed and breakfasts, a campsite, toilets, pubs and a beach café. Arriva buses run from the Runswick Bay Hotel back to Staithes, Saltburn and Middlesbrough, as well as ahead to Sandsend and Whitby.

If the tide is in, the best course of action is to wait for it to recede, as any attempt to detour inland will be inconvenient and time-consuming.

Note that onward progress might be blocked across **Runswick Sands** by very high tides, so time your arrival to avoid high water. The Cleveland Way is routed along the sandy beach, passing the blue-and-white Runswick Bay Sailing Club building at the far end. ◄

Continue past a crumbling cliff at **Hob Holes** to find a river valley cutting through flaky beds of shale.

Head inland through this valley as marked, scrambling up crumbling slopes of shale. A flight of 95 steps is followed by another flight of 160 steps up a bushy slope, out of the valley and along the top of High Cliff, around 100m (330ft).

Note that the line of a disused railway lies a little further inland. The cliff path is pushed inland a little by a small gully choked with bushes. Turn left to follow a track through the farming hamlet of **Kettleness**. Apart from the first white building, keep seawards of all other buildings to pick up the cliff path as marked later.

After leaving Runswick Bay, the Cleveland Way climbs towards Kettleness

The bare, rugged headland of Kettle Ness was once worked for alum, jet and ironstone. The previous village of **Kettleness** slumped into the sea in 1829. There was no loss of life, since the slump was gradual and the inhabitants were safely loaded onto a ship that was waiting for a consignment of alum. The alum works were destroyed, along with the village, but the slump exposed more shale to be quarried, so a new works was built and operations began again within two years. There are no facilities in the village for walkers.

After following the grassy cliff-top path around the **Kettle Ness** headland, note that the **dismantled railway** is close to hand again. Watch it carefully to see it disappear into a tunnel. ▶ Keep following the cliff path onwards.

The tunnel (or tunnels, since there are actually two) was cut after the original coastal railway was lost in a cliff fall.

157

A notice fixed to a gatepost gives distances back to Helmsley and ahead to Filey, while a signpost later points inland to the Fox and Hounds at nearby **Goldsborough** if food or drink is needed.

The cliff path later drops down a wooded slope into a valley by means of steeply pitched steps and a stairway. It can be slippery underfoot, so take care. The route lands on the disused railway trackbed, close to the mouth of the Sandsend Tunnel, which is 1.5km (1 mile) long. Turn left to walk along the old trackbed, through a cutting and along an embankment, passing old alum workings at **Sandsend Ness**, while looking ahead to Sandsend and Whitby. There are nature trail marker posts along the way. After a short wooded stretch, drop down almost 50 steps on the left into a car park below the old station site. Walk along a promenade path beside the A174 road into **Sandsend**.

SANDSEND AND EAST ROW

These two little villages grew closer together when cottages were built for alum workers. The industry continued for over 250 years in Mulgrave Woods and around Sandsend Ness, ceasing operation in 1867. The coastal railway came past the villages in 1855, bored through headlands and straddled valleys on lofty viaducts, bringing with it increased prosperity through tourist developments. Building projects made the two villages into one. The railway line closed in 1958, but the sandy beach is close enough to Whitby for the village to remain popular with local people and visitors.

Sandsend and neighbouring East Row offer accommodation, a shop, toilets, pub, restaurants, café and a beach shop. There are regular Arriva buses back along the coast to Runswick Bay, Staithes, Skelton, Guisborough and Middlesbrough, as well as ahead to Whitby.

STAGE 7

Sandsend to Robin Hood's Bay

Start	Sandsend (NZ 860 129)
Finish	Bay Hotel, Robin Hood's Bay (NZ 953 048)
Distance	16.5km (10¼ miles)
Time	5hr
Terrain	An initial road walk and urban walking, then a reasonably easy cliff path with only a few short, steep ascents and descents.
Maps	OS Landranger 94, OS Explorer OL27, Harvey Cleveland Way
Refreshments	Plenty of pubs, cafés and restaurants at Whitby. Pub and café at Saltwick Bay. Pubs, cafés and restaurants at Robin Hood's Bay.
Public transport	Arriva buses link Whitby, Sandsend, Runswick Bay, Staithes, Skelton, Guisborough and Middlesbrough. Arriva buses also link Whitby, Guisborough and Middlesbrough with Robin Hood's Bay and Scarborough. Northern trains link Whitby with Kildale and Middlesbrough. Yorkshire Coastliner buses link Whitby with Pickering, York and Leeds.

Plenty of people enjoy the easy stroll between Sandsend and Whitby, while the roller-coaster cliff path between Whitby and Robin Hood's Bay is also a popular choice for a day's walk. Few long-distance walkers would rush through Whitby without spending a while exploring the narrow streets and bustling harbour. Although the din of amusement arcades and the constant mewling of gulls can be an assault on the ears, there is plenty of interest in this old whaling town. Even when the time comes to leave town, Whitby Abbey, perched high above the town, offers yet another distraction. Whatever happens, allow time in the evening for exploring Robin Hood's Bay, where a delightful heap of houses clings to a steep slope and the last pub, the Bay Hotel, practically sits in the sea!

Cross the bridge between **Sandsend** and **East Row** and follow the main A174 road gently uphill, drifting inland from the sand and shingle beach. If the tide is out, the beach can be followed all the way to Whitby, but the Cleveland Way stays on dry land and passes Whitby Golf Club by road.

map continues on
page 163

Soon after passing the clubhouse, a track on the left is signposted as the Cleveland Way and leads down towards **Upgang Beach**. Walk beneath a golfer's footbridge and turn right to follow a tarmac path across a slope, although there are plenty of other paths available.

Staying on top of the slope leads past a series of hotels along North Promenade and North Terrace, as well as a cliff lift and the Whitby Pavilion. A prominent memorial to Captain Cook stands beside a famous whalebone arch.

CAPTAIN COOK

After moving to Whitby from Staithes in 1747 James Cook was an apprentice seaman, lodging in an attic belonging to his Quaker master John Walker. Apprentices learned the art of navigation and seamanship through lessons and practical experience on coal-carriers sailing to and from London. Cook's naval career commenced in 1755 and lasted almost 25 years until his untimely death in Hawaii in 1779. It is no doubt a testimony to Whitby's shipbuilding expertise that four of Captain Cook's ships were built in the town: *Endeavour*, *Resolution*, *Discovery* and *Adventure*. There is a replica of *Endeavour* in the harbour, where it can be boarded and inspected. It often sails out of the harbour for short trips. The Captain Cook Memorial Museum on Grape Lane charts the life and times of this remarkable explorer. There is an entrance charge, tel 01947 601900, www.cookmuseumwhitby.co.uk.

WHITBY WHALERS

Whitby developed greatly as a town from the mid-18th to mid-19th centuries as its fishing fleets turned to whaling. Whalers spent months at sea and did not always return with a catch. Whale blubber was highly prized, the oil rendered from it giving a bright, soot-free light when burned. Women of the era would have more than enough reason to curse their whalebone corsets, but the whaling trade allowed the town to prosper immensely. The whalebone arch was presented to the town by Norway, suggesting that the Whitby whalers always disposed of every last part of their catch!

Walk through the whalebone arch to find steps winding down a steep slope to the harbour at **Whitby**. Head inland to cross the Swing Bridge spanning the tidal mouth of the River Esk. Alternatively, spend more time wandering around a veritable maze of narrow streets on both sides of the harbour to discover more about the heritage of the town. Bram Stoker would have been hard-pressed to find a better town to bring Dracula ashore, and as a result, there is an annual Whitby Goth Weekend!

Facilities in **Whitby** include all types of accommodation, including a youth hostel and nearby campsite. There are banks with ATMs, a post office, toilets, and plenty of pubs, restaurants, cafés and takeaways. The tourist information centre is near Endeavour Wharf, tel 01723 383636. The most useful bus services are the Arriva buses back to Sandsend, Runswick Bay, Staithes, Skelton, Guisborough and Middlesbrough; Arriva buses back to Guisborough and Middlesbrough; and Arriva buses ahead to Robin Hood's Bay and Scarborough. Yorkshire Coastliner buses link Whitby with Pickering, York and Leeds. Northern trains link Whitby with Kildale and Middlesbrough.

A cobbled road leads to the famous 199 steps leading up and out of Whitby

WHITBY ABBEY

St Hilda founded Whitby Abbey in the year 657. According to legend, fossilised ammonites were snakes turned to stone by St Hilda! The Danes destroyed the abbey in 867, another foundation of 1078 was also unsuccessful, and much of what is seen today dates from the 12th century. However, the original abbey was founded in time to host the Synod of Whitby in the year 664. At this synod the Celtic and Roman Christian traditions, separated during the Dark Ages, settled some of the differences that each had accrued over the years, and agreed a method for calculating the movable feast of Easter. The abbey is also famous for one of its early lay brothers, Caedmon, who was inspired to sing in a dream one night, and whose words form the earliest English Christian written verse. There is an entrance charge, tel 01947 603568.

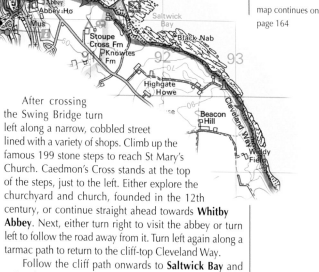

map continues on
page 164

After crossing the Swing Bridge turn left along a narrow, cobbled street lined with a variety of shops. Climb up the famous 199 stone steps to reach St Mary's Church. Caedmon's Cross stands at the top of the steps, just to the left. Either explore the churchyard and church, founded in the 12th century, or continue straight ahead towards **Whitby Abbey**. Next, either turn right to visit the abbey or turn left to follow the road away from it. Turn left again along a tarmac path to return to the cliff-top Cleveland Way.

Follow the cliff path onwards to **Saltwick Bay** and enjoy the open coastal scenery again. **Saltwick Nab** is a prominent humpbacked headland, but one that largely results from the quarrying of alum shales. There is access to the beach if required, otherwise walk along the road through the Whitby Holiday Village where there is a campsite, shop, pub and café. Just as the road leaves the site a Cleveland Way signpost points left along a grassy cliff path. There is a view down to the isolated sea stack of **Black Nab**, which was also formed by alum-shale quarrying. The twisted wreckage of the *Admiral Von Tromp*, which ran aground in 1976, can be seen near the beach.

Pass from field to field using kissing gates, keep to the seaward side of a foghorn, but follow a path on the landward side of a lighthouse. Climb higher along the cliff path to around 90m (295ft) above sea level. The path basically rolls along, rising and falling fairly gently, sometimes with short flights of steps, with rugged cliffs down

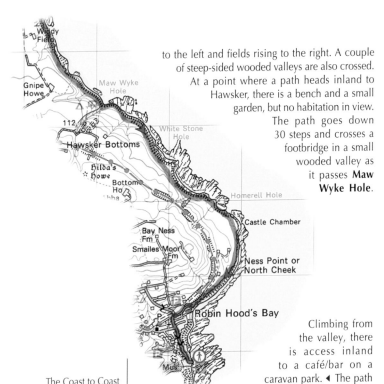

to the left and fields rising to the right. A couple of steep-sided wooded valleys are also crossed. At a point where a path heads inland to Hawsker, there is a bench and a small garden, but no habitation in view. The path goes down 30 steps and crosses a footbridge in a small wooded valley as it passes **Maw Wyke Hole**.

The Coast to Coast Walk, last seen on the highest part of the North York Moors, re-joins the Cleveland Way.

Climbing from the valley, there is access inland to a café/bar on a caravan park. ◄ The path continues, crossing a couple of small, stone-slab footbridges, and later crosses a couple more footbridges as it crosses a gentle valley at Rain Dale. Enjoy views back along the cliff coast.

Walk around **Ness Point** to see Robin Hood's Bay, but only after passing below the old coastguard hut and entering the Rocket Post Field. The path runs to the top end of the village, then along Mount Pleasant North. Turn left at a junction near the Grosvenor Hotel and walk down the B1447 road to a roundabout beside the Victoria Hotel.

Continue down a steep and narrow road, with over 100 steps alongside, winding past the jumbled houses and cottages of **Robin Hood's Bay**, to reach the rocky shore at a stout sea wall that holds the village in place.

Robin Hood's Bay is a delightful old village with a tradition of smuggling

The Bay Hotel bears a plaque marking the end of the Coast to Coast Walk, but the Cleveland Way is still good for a couple more days of splendid walking.

ROBIN HOOD'S BAY

This charming and curiously complex village has a history of smuggling during which the villagers often engaged in hostilities with the revenue men. Local folk claim that a bolt of silk could be passed through secret cupboards and doorways from the shore to the top of the village without seeing the light of day. They also tell of an incident when smugglers and revenue men waged a pitched battle in the bay, and it was possible to read newsprint at night from the flash of gun-powder. One thing seems certain – that Robin Hood never had any association with the village. The Bay Hotel rises straight from the rocky, fossil-rich shore, and has had one ship wrecked against its wall and another poke its bowsprit straight through a window. The National Trust operates the Old Coastguard Station Visitor Centre opposite, tel 01947 885900.

Facilities include plenty of accommodation, including a nearby youth hostel and campsite, a post office, toilets, pubs, restaurants, cafés and a few shops. Arriva buses run from the top of the village ahead to Scarborough, as well as back towards Whitby, Guisborough and Middlesbrough.

Looking back to Robin Hood's Bay and its delightful stack of houses

STAGE 8

Robin Hood's Bay to Scarborough

Start	Bay Hotel, Robin Hood's Bay (NZ 953 048)
Finish	North Bay, Scarborough (TA 037 897)
Distance	22km (13¾ miles)
Time	6hr 30min
Terrain	Gentle cliff walking followed by field paths to Ravenscar. The cliff path onwards features several short ascents and descents, with some short, steep slopes. Easy promenade walk at the finish.
Maps	OS Landrangers 94 and 101, OS Explorer OL27, Harvey Cleveland Way
Refreshments	Pub and café at Ravenscar. Pub near Hayburn Wyke. Pub at Old Scalby Mills. Plenty of pubs, restaurants, cafés and takeaways around Scarborough.
Public transport	Arriva buses link Robin Hood's Bay and Scarborough, as well as running back to Whitby, Guisborough and Middlesbrough. East Yorkshire buses link Ravenscar and Scarborough, except Sunday. East Yorkshire buses link Old Scalby Mills with Scarborough, except Sunday. There is also a miniature railway from the Sea Life Centre to Peasholm Park in Scarborough.

As Robin Hood's Bay recedes from view, the cliff-top village of Ravenscar is seen ahead. An entire resort was once planned on top of Old Peak. Hardly any of it was built, but some of the roads that were laid out are still clearly visible. Sloping cliffs covered with thick woodland scrub make ideal wildlife habitats, particularly around Beast Cliff. There is an attractive boulder beach with a small waterfall at Hayburn Wyke. Beyond Cloughton Wyke the Cleveland Way leaves the North York Moors National Park, but the cliff coastline is attractive all the way to Old Scalby Mills. Ahead lies the busy seaside resort of Scarborough, with its headland dominated by a ruined castle.

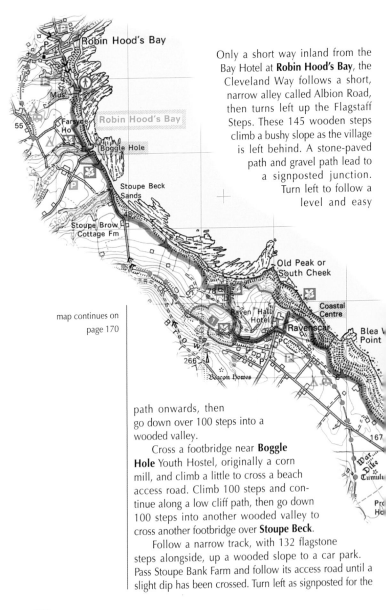

Only a short way inland from the Bay Hotel at **Robin Hood's Bay**, the Cleveland Way follows a short, narrow alley called Albion Road, then turns left up the Flagstaff Steps. These 145 wooden steps climb a bushy slope as the village is left behind. A stone-paved path and gravel path lead to a signposted junction. Turn left to follow a level and easy

map continues on
page 170

path onwards, then go down over 100 steps into a wooded valley.

Cross a footbridge near **Boggle Hole** Youth Hostel, originally a corn mill, and climb a little to cross a beach access road. Climb 100 steps and continue along a low cliff path, then go down 100 steps into another wooded valley to cross another footbridge over **Stoupe Beck**.

Follow a narrow track, with 132 flagstone steps alongside, up a wooded slope to a car park. Pass Stoupe Bank Farm and follow its access road until a slight dip has been crossed. Turn left as signposted for the

Cleveland Way, picking up the cliff path again. Views back along the coast reveal the village of Robin Hood's Bay becoming distant, while ahead the village of Ravenscar draws nearer. The path is broad and grassy, running around 60m (200ft) above sea level. It goes through small gates and crosses four footbridges – the last of which is flanked by dozens of steps – while heading inland.

Follow the path further inland past the ruins of the Peak Alum Works. Turn left along a farm track made of concrete strips, and soon afterwards fork right up a clear path flanked by broom and gorse bushes. The path rises through woods and continues along a track studded with bricks that were made locally and stamped with the name **Ravenscar**. Walk to a road junction at the entrance gate of the Raven Hall Country House Hotel, near a visitor centre, around 190m (625ft).

The Romans built a signal station at **Ravenscar** more or less where the Raven Hall Hotel now stands. Alum mining was a profitable occupation in the area, leaving the cliffs around Old Peak looking rather bare. In the 1890s there was a grand scheme to create a tourist resort here, but despite a road system and drains being laid, very few investors bought plots or built properties, and the scheme ground to a halt in the 1920s. Facilities include the hotel, as well as other accommodation and a campsite. There are toilets, a pub, tearoom and a National Trust Visitor Centre, tel 01723 870138. East Yorkshire buses link Ravenscar with Scarborough, except Sunday.

Walk along Station Road, then turn left as signposted along a wide and stony track to regain the cliff path. Follow the grassy cliff path roughly on a level. ▶ Descend a short way to enjoy views across a deep and wonderfully rugged hollow in the cliff face at **Blea Wyke Point**. After passing the Ravenscar Radar Station, the path runs around 150m (490ft) above sea level and passes the wild

A signpost points inland to a nearby tearoom.

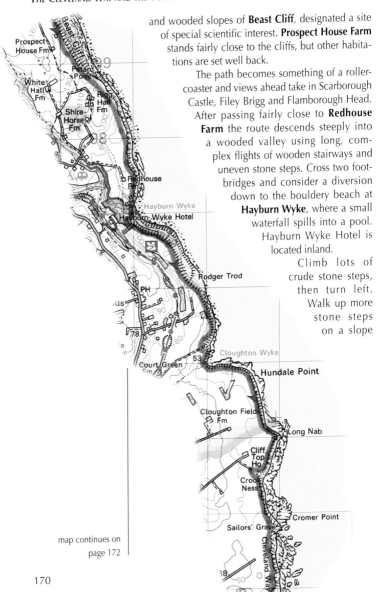

and wooded slopes of **Beast Cliff**, designated a site of special scientific interest. **Prospect House Farm** stands fairly close to the cliffs, but other habitations are set well back.

The path becomes something of a roller-coaster and views ahead take in Scarborough Castle, Filey Brigg and Flamborough Head. After passing fairly close to **Redhouse Farm** the route descends steeply into a wooded valley using long, complex flights of wooden stairways and uneven stone steps. Cross two footbridges and consider a diversion down to the bouldery beach at **Hayburn Wyke**, where a small waterfall spills into a pool. Hayburn Wyke Hotel is located inland.

Climb lots of crude stone steps, then turn left. Walk up more stone steps on a slope

map continues on
page 172

A slender waterfall spills into a rock pool on the beach at Hayburn Wyke

covered with intriguingly twisted corkscrew oaks and rhododendron. Watch for a junction of paths and keep right, crossing another footbridge and moving further inland through the woods along the clearest path.

Climb to the left up yet more stone steps and turn left at the top. Climb even further to leave the woods and continue along the top of the wooded slope, looking back towards the bay. When a grassy crest is reached at **Rodger Trod** there is a valley down to the right and the cliff coast to the left. Views ahead suggest a gentle descent, but the route is more like a switchback around the bay of **Cloughton Wyke**, with dozens more steps up and down some of the slopes.

An easier cliff-top path crosses a footbridge and continues around **Hundale Point**, taking in two more

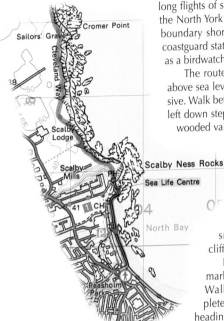

long flights of steps. The Cleveland Way leaves the North York Moors National Park at a field boundary shortly before reaching the former coastguard station on **Long Nab**. It now serves as a birdwatching station.

The route continues barely 40m (130ft) above sea level, but the cliffs remain impressive. Walk between cliffs and fields, then turn left down steps to cross a concrete path in a wooded valley at **Crook Ness**. Climb more steps and continue along the cliff path. There are quite a few little ups and downs and the route passes the Sailors' Grave on **Cromer Point**. There is no actual grave; the name refers to a small and rugged bite in the cliffs.

Later, a signpost pointing inland marks the start of the Tabular Hills Walk, allowing walkers to complete an immense circular walk by heading inland back to Helmsley. The

A view around North Bay from the flowery Queens Parade in Scarborough

Cleveland Way, however, continues to hug the cliff coast to Scalby Nab. Either walk around this final promontory or cut behind it and follow a path, using steps to descend. Two flights, totalling 75 stone steps, lead down a bushy slope to reach a footbridge. The Old Scalby Mills pub is immediately to hand.

There are buses into Scarborough from here and the Sea Life Sanctuary, www.visitsealife.com/scarborough, is an immediate distraction. A miniature railway tempts walkers to take a ride, but it is simple enough to walk along North Bay Promenade to continue. The promenade is traffic-free and leads to the outskirts of **Scarborough**, where the popular Peasholm Park lies just inland from **North Bay**.

SCARBOROUGH

The emergence of Scarborough as a holiday resort can be traced to the promotion of its spa waters. In 1626 a local doctor extolled the benefits of drinking the water, making so many claims about its curative properties that one must suspect quackery! However, visitors flocked to the town and before long the benefits of sea air and sea bathing were also being promoted. So enthusiastic were the crowds of holidaymakers that more and more facilities had to be built to cater for them. The arrival of the railway in 1845 boosted the tourism trade and the town remains a busy and bustling place to this day.

Facilities around Scarborough include a wide range of accommodation options, from splendid hotels to humble bed-and-breakfasts, as well as a youth hostel at Scalby Mills and nearby campsites. There are banks with ATMs, post offices, toilets, and an abundance of pubs, restaurants, cafés and takeaways to suit all tastes, although in many cases it's 'chips with everything'. As a shopping centre Scarborough has the greatest choice of any place visited in this guidebook. The tourist information centre is on Burniston Road, near Peasholm Park, tel 01723 818111, **www.discoveryorkshirecoast.com/scarborough**.

Trains run to a number of destinations throughout the country, including to Filey, Hull, York and Leeds. Yorkshire Coastliner buses link Scarborough with York and Leeds. Arriva buses link Scarborough with Robin Hood's Bay, Whitby, Guisborough and Middlesbrough. East Yorkshire buses link Scarborough with Scalby Mills and the Sea Life Sanctuary. East Yorkshire buses link Scarborough and Filey, as well as heading inland to Helmsley, where the Cleveland Way starts.

STAGE 9
Scarborough to Filey

Start	North Bay, Scarborough (TA 037 897)
Finish	Coble Landing, Filey (TA 120 809)
Distance	18km (11 miles)
Time	5hr 15min
Terrain	Urban walking gives way to a rugged, wooded slope followed by fairly straightforward cliff walking.
Maps	OS Landranger 101, OS Explorer 301, Harvey Cleveland Way
Refreshments	Plenty of refreshment options around Scarborough. Beach hut and surf shop at Cayton Bay. Plenty of pubs, restaurants and cafés around Filey.
Public transport	East Yorkshire bus services run all around Scarborough, while East Yorkshire buses 120 and 121 operate between Scarborough and Filey. Northern trains run between Scarborough and Filey.

The Cleveland Way is not waymarked or signposted through Scarborough. Indeed, some writers have suggested getting a bus through town rather than walking, but this seems remiss given that Scarborough has plenty of interest that is best discovered on foot. Walkers might opt to head straight through the town centre, or follow Marine Drive around the headland, but for those who would like to appreciate some of Scarborough's history and heritage a route is offered below that takes in a few of its more prominent features. Once clear of the town, wooded slopes and fairly easy cliff walking leads onwards to Filey Brigg. For some obscure reason the Cleveland Way ends in the middle of nowhere, before reaching the impressive headland of Filey Brigg, and walkers find themselves embarking on the course of the Yorkshire Wolds Way in order to reach the end of the day's walk at Filey.

There is no 'official' waymarked route for the Cleveland Way from **North Bay** through **Scarborough**. The simplest option smacks a little of 'cheating', which is to catch one of the open-top Suncruiser buses from North Bay to South Bay. The simplest alter- native on foot is to walk along the promenade, first following Royal Albert Drive, continu- ing along Marine Drive around the headland at the foot of **Castle Cliff** to reach the **Old Harbour**. Follow the busy promenade beside Foreshore Road to con- tinue around **South Bay**.

map continues
on page 177

Those who wish to see more of Scarborough's his- tory and heritage should leave Royal Albert Drive and follow paths up a slope to walk along Queens Parade and Blenheim Terrace. Unless a visit to the town centre appeals, turn right at the Norbreck Hotel and seek out St Mary's Church, where visitors search the churchyard for Anne Brontë's grave. **Scarborough Castle** is easily reached from the church, and various paths and flights of steps can be used to descend to a roundabout near the harbour.

> Bronze Age settlers are thought to have been the first to fortify the headland at Scarborough. The Romans operated a signal station on a line of sight linked with other coastal signal stations at Ravenscar and Filey Brigg. In the 12th century **Scarborough Castle** was built on the headland. The castle withstood a 20-day siege during the Pilgrimage of Grace in 1536, but surrendered after a year-long siege dur- ing the Civil War in 1645. The ruins of the castle can be visited while exploring the town. There is an entrance charge, tel 01723 372451.

175

Looking across South Bay to Scarborough and its castle

After following the busy promenade beside Foreshore Road, the imposing Grand Hotel rises inland. There is a fine geology **museum** at the Rotunda, which can be seen from the promenade through the arches of the Spa Bridge, near the hotel.

The Spa complex lies at the end of a road on **South Bay**, and a clear path continues along the top of a sea wall. Take careful note of the tide and the state of the sea. Notices warn that high seas can break over the sea wall. If it looks dangerous to proceed, there are plenty of paths and roads at a higher level that can be used instead, and walking through the South Cliff Gardens and Holbeck Gardens is an attractive option.

If following the sea wall, the route soon passes the 'Star Disk'. It doesn't look much during the day, but anyone visiting at night-time will see a number of stars and constellations illuminated over a wide area of the ground, representing the night sky. Beyond, a great bulge of landslip material has been landscaped. A clear track signposted for Filey climbs towards a car park at the end of Sea Cliff Road. The Holbeck Hall Hotel once stood nearby.

map continues on page 178

The **Holbeck Hall Hotel** was built as a private residence in 1880 and later converted into a hotel. Unfortunately the ground beneath the building was unstable and began to slump on 3 June 1993 – an event that was

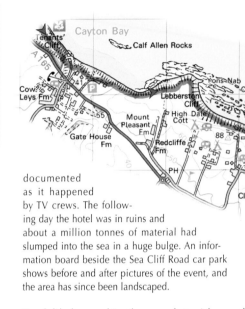

documented
as it happened
by TV crews. The follow-
ing day the hotel was in ruins and
about a million tonnes of material had
slumped into the sea in a huge bulge. An information board beside the Sea Cliff Road car park
shows before and after pictures of the event, and
the area has since been landscaped.

Turn left before reaching the car park, to pick up and
follow a path across a wooded slope. Keep to the 'rough'
around the edge of a **golf course**, close to a crumbling
clay cliff that displays numerous landslips. Walk round
a small headland at **White Nab**, then turn left down 45
stone steps. Turn right up a track, then turn left to leave it
and follow a path that soon crosses a duckboard. Follow
a grassy path beside the edge of a woodland at the top of
Frank Cliff. When houses are reached near **Knipe Point**,
turn right to follow a path inland, then turn left along the
A165 road.

Osgodby is virtually a suburb of Scarborough, but
the Cleveland Way avoids the built-up sprawl as much as
possible. Turn left down flights of wooden steps, counting well over 100 of them. The Cleveland Way wanders
across a wooded slope with occasional shorter flights of
steps. Keep an eye on route markers, as some paths lead
off-route down to the beach. ◂

Geologists might
like to detour to
Cornelian Bay in
the hope of picking
semi-precious stones
from the beach.

While walking past **Tenants Cliff**, note the Second World War pillboxes, some of which have toppled from the crumbling clay cliffs on which they were built. Keep right to climb a steep, stone-pitched path, then turn left and descend to a beach access road above **Cayton Bay**, noting that there is a beach shop just off-route. Cross the road and climb from it, shortly reaching another road that leads inland to a surf shop that sells sweets and ice cream. Follow the path seawards of a cliff-top cottage and a row of houses.

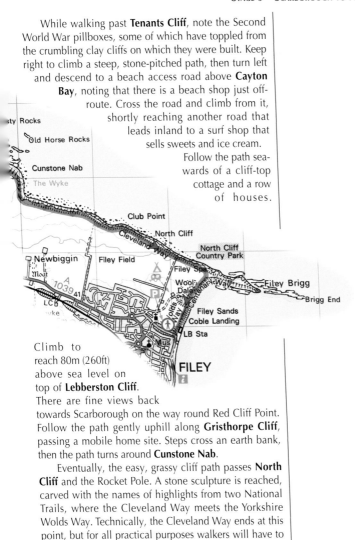

Climb to reach 80m (260ft) above sea level on top of **Lebberston Cliff**. There are fine views back towards Scarborough on the way round Red Cliff Point. Follow the path gently uphill along **Gristhorpe Cliff**, passing a mobile home site. Steps cross an earth bank, then the path turns around **Cunstone Nab**.

Eventually, the easy, grassy cliff path passes **North Cliff** and the Rocket Pole. A stone sculpture is reached, carved with the names of highlights from two National Trails, where the Cleveland Way meets the Yorkshire Wolds Way. Technically, the Cleveland Way ends at this point, but for all practical purposes walkers will have to continue to nearby Filey. First, walk out onto the grassy crest of **Filey Brigg** and enjoy views of the rocky tidal reef projecting into the sea.

FILEY BRIGG

The grassy top of Filey Brigg has been crumbling steadily over the centuries and will one day be gone, leaving only the hard calcareous gritstone bedrock beneath. A Roman signal station and 12th-century castle have already been lost as the clay cliffs have crumbled, and walkers are now asked not to continue along the badly worn and dangerous clay ridge down to the rocky slabs of Brigg End. To visit the end of the Brigg, you should do it by walking along Filey Sands when the tide is out. Bear in mind that the rocks are covered in slippery seaweed and big waves sometimes break across them without warning. There is an emergency telephone for those who find themselves marooned out on the point or spot anyone in obvious difficulty or danger.

With care, at low water, the rocky end of Filey Brigg can be visited

Follow an easy, grassy cliff-top path through the **Filey Country Park**. Over 100 steps drop into the little **Wool Dale** and over 100 more steps climb from it. The path continues above the Filey Sailing Club, then goes down a zigzag path featuring well over 100 more steps on a wooded slope into Church Ravine. Just to the left, at the bottom, is the **Coble Landing**, where fishing boats are brought up from the beach. ◄

'Coble' is pronounced 'cobble'.

Walkers are now already following the Yorkshire Wolds Way, which can be used to enter **Filey** by climbing steps and a path inland from a toilet block. Follow Queen Street past the town council offices, then turn left along Reynolds Street. Turn right along Mitford Street and left along Union Street. Turn right along Station Avenue, which leads past a bus station on its way to a railway station – for the journey back home.

A view of the crumbling headland of Filey Brigg from the Filey Country Park

FILEY

Filey is a little fishing town that has turned its attention to tourism. On the Coble Landing, fishing boats lie on trailers beside amusement arcades, as if the transition is not yet complete. The town is fairly small but supports a good variety of services, whether walkers are at the end of the Yorkshire Wolds Way or the Cleveland Way, or even if they are starting from Filey.

Facilities include a range of accommodation and a nearby campsite. There are banks with ATMs, a post office, toilets, plenty of pubs, restaurants, cafés and takeaways, as well as shops. The museum should be visited by anyone wanting a potted history of the town. There is a tourist information centre on John Street, tel 01723 383636, **www.discoveryorkshirecoast.com/filey**. East Yorkshire buses regularly link Filey with Scarborough as well as Bridlington and distant Hull. Yorkshire Coastliner buses regularly link Filey with Malton, York and Leeds. Trains run from Filey to Scarborough and Hull.

THE WALKING PARSON

The Rev Arthur Cooper was born in 1827 and took up walking as a means of getting around his parish while he was a curate in Durham. At the age of 60, shortly after taking an appointment in the parish of Filey, he decided to walk from Filey to Rome. He practised by walking from Filey to London in less than a week, taking the Sunday service before leaving Filey and returning to take the following Sunday service. This was simply to prove to himself that he was capable of covering long distances. He then walked from Filey to Rome in only seven weeks, declaring, 'Good-bye all ye vampires of modern travel. Good-bye insolent cab men and tip-loving porters. Good-bye misdirected luggage and dusty railway carriages.' Several more European treks followed, mostly along car-free roads.

Cooper also wrote books and gave talks about his journeys. Although teetotal, he was in the habit of stomping into pubs and ordering glasses of whisky, which he poured into his shoes while still wearing them, declaring, 'It makes the foot and sock and shoe all pliable together.' At the time of his death in 1920, at the grand old age of 93, opinions were divided as to whether he was a complete eccentric or the greatest British walker of his time, or both. He can make the rest of us, even after walking 400km (250 miles) around Yorkshire, feel like mere novices!

Coble Landing at Filey, where boats are brought up alongside amusement arcades

APPENDIX A
Useful contacts

National Trail information
Yorkshire Wolds Way
www.nationaltrail.co.uk/
yorkshire-wolds-way

Cleveland Way
www.nationaltrail.co.uk/cleveland-way

Trail Officer
North York Moors National Park
The Old Vicarage
Bondgate
Helmsley
YO62 5BP
tel 01439 772700

Tourist information centres

Yorkshire Wolds Way National Trail
Hull
Paragon Interchange
Hull
HU1 3UF
tel 01482 300306

Humber Bridge
North Bank Viewing Area
Ferriby Road
Hessle
HU13 0LN
tel 01482 640852

Beverley
Champney Road
Beverley
HU17 8HE
tel 01482 391672

Filey
John Street
Filey
YO14 9DW
tel 01723 383636

Tabular Hills Walk
Scarborough
Burniston Road
Scarborough
YO12 6PF
tel 01723 383636

Cleveland Way National Trail
Sutton Bank
National Park Centre
Sutton Bank
Thirsk
YO7 2EH
tel 01845 597426

Great Ayton
Discovery Centre
Great Ayton
TS9 6NB
tel 01642 723268

Staithes
Gateway Centre
Whitegate Close
Staithes
TS13 5BB
tel 01947 844100

Whitby
Langborne Road
Whitby
YO21 1YN
tel 01723 383636

Ravenscar
National Trust Coastal Centre
Ravenscar
tel 01723 870138

Scarborough
Burniston Road
Scarborough
YO12 6PF
tel 01723 383636

Filey
John Street
Filey
YO14 9DW
tel 01723 383636

North York Moors National Park

National Park Office
The Old Vicarage
Bondgate
Helmsley
YO62 5BP
tel 01439 772700
www.northyorkmoors.org.uk

National Park Centre
Sutton BankThirsk
YO7 2EH
tel 01845 597426

Getting to Yorkshire

By air
Leeds-Bradford Airport
www.leedsbradfordairport.co.uk

Manchester Airport
www.manchesterairport.co.uk

Teesside International Airport
www.teessideinternational.com

By ferry
P&O Ferries
www.poferries.com

By rail
Hull Trains
www.hulltrains.co.uk

First Transpennine Express
www.tpexpress.co.uk

By coach
Eurolines
www.eurolines.com

National Express
www.nationalexpress.com

Getting around Yorkshire

By train
Northern
www.northernrailway.co.uk

By bus
Yorkshire Coastliner
www.transdevbus.co.uk/york

East Yorkshire
www.eastyorkshirebuses.co.uk

Arriva
www.arrivabus.co.uk

Traveline
tel 0871 2002233
www.traveline.info

NOTES

NOTES

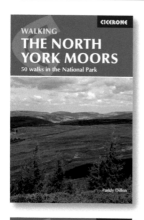
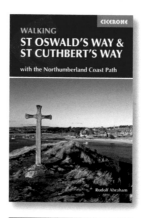
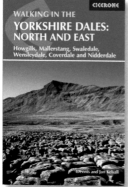
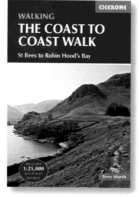

The Great Outdoors

DIGITAL SUBSCRIPTION
£37.99
FOR A YEAR

- Save 41%* off the cover price
- Substantial savings on the newsstand price and print subscriptions
- Instant access wherever you are, even if you are offline
- Back issues at your fingertips

Downloading **The Great Outdoors** to your digital device is easy, just follow the steps below:

1 Download the App from the App Store

2 Open the App, click on 'subscriptions' and choose an annual subscription

3 Download the latest issue and enjoy

The digital edition is also available on

*Discounts calculated on the full cover price

LISTING OF CICERONE GUIDES

For full information on all our guides,
books and eBooks, visit our website:
www.cicerone.co.uk

Explore the world with Cicerone

walking • trekking • mountaineering • climbing • mountain biking • cycling • via ferratas • scrambling • trail running • skills and techniques

For over 50 years, Cicerone have built up an outstanding collection of nearly 400 guides, inspiring all sorts of amazing experiences.

www.cicerone.co.uk – where adventures begin

- Our **website** is a treasure-trove for every outdoor adventurer. You can buy books or read inspiring articles and trip reports, get technical advice, check for updates, and view videos, photographs and mapping for routes and treks.

- **Register this book** or any other Cicerone guide in your member's library on our website and you can choose to automatically access updates and GPX files for your books, if available.

- Our **fortnightly newsletters** will update you on new publications and articles and keep you informed of other news and events. You can also follow us on Facebook, Twitter and Instagram.

We hope you have enjoyed using this guidebook. If you have any comments you would like to share, please contact us using the form on our website or via email, so that we can provide the best experience for future customers.

CICERONE

Juniper House, Murley Moss Business Village, Oxenholme Road, Kendal LA9 7RL

✉ info@cicerone.co.uk   cicerone.co.uk 🔲🔲🔲